No Fear

Growing up in a
risk averse society

No Fear

Growing up in a
risk averse society

TIM GILL

CALOUSTE GULBENKIAN FOUNDATION

Published by
Calouste Gulbenkian Foundation
United Kingdom Branch
98 Portland Place
London W1B 1ET
Tel: 020 7908 7604
E-mail: info@gulbenkian.org.uk
Website: www.gulbenkian.org.uk

The views expressed in this book are those of the author, not necessarily
those of the Calouste Gulbenkian Foundation.

ISBN 978 1 903080 08 5

British Library Cataloguing-in-Publication Data
A catalogue record for this book is available from the British Library

Designed by Helen Swansbourne
Printed by Berforts Group, Stevenage

Distributed by Central Books Ltd, 99 Wallis Road, London E9 5LN
Tel: 0845 458 9911, Fax: 0845 458 9912
E-mail: orders@centralbooks.com
Website: www.centralbooks.com

Cover: Lucas Kimber by Nils Norman, 2006.
Title page: Tunstall Forest, Suffolk, 2006. Photo: Virginia Sullivan.

Contents

Preface

You don't need a vivid imagination, or a very good memory, to recall the last horrific incident involving a child or young person. I shudder at the thought; but I shudder, too, because I know that the tragedy, however caused, will be followed by the inevitable witch-hunt and knee-jerk reaction with little regard for long-term consequences. Our commentators and policymakers, whipped up by a sensationalist media and public demand, all too often act first and think second. And in the heat of the moment, any sense of balance or proportionality can be lost.

The Government's *Every Child Matters* agenda has put the well-being of our nation's children to the fore: their health and safety as well as their opportunity to contribute, enjoy and achieve. That is as it should be. But we need to ensure that the promotion of one strand of this agenda does not become the enemy of the others; that 'safety first' does not drive out the opportunities children should have for experiment and development; and that our desire to defend young people against some very real dangers does not lead us into a sanitised world in which creativity and personal growth are stifled.

The Calouste Gulbenkian Foundation has a long tradition of influential work on children's issues and our involvement reflects our core aim of seeking to bring about lasting, beneficial change in the experiences that people – particularly young people – have in life. The Gulbenkian approach has always been to look beyond fashion and pose the questions some wish were left unasked. At the same time, we have always sought to shed a positive light on the issues of the day and put forward practical solutions that go beyond conventional wisdom.

More than once we have concluded that trends in education and child policy have been going in the wrong direction and we have set out to help develop new thinking and support others in advocating a change in approach. The ultimately successful ten-year campaign for a Children's Commissioner is a classic example of Gulbenkian Foundation work. Our Commission on Children and Violence, chaired by Sir William

Utting in 1995, looked at the quality of children's lives from a different angle; examining the extent of violence involving children and why children become violent, the Commission put forward recommendations aimed at reducing the problem in the future.

This report, focusing on the freedoms children enjoy and how those have been diminished, maintains that tradition. Working with Tim Gill, one of Britain's foremost experts in child play, the report takes a robust but responsible approach to risk in childhood. Nor is play new for us: the Foundation once funded the Children's Play Council (then headed by Tim Gill) to promote child-friendly streets. The project was the first step in CPC's campaign for home zones that led in time to a £30 million government programme and the hundred or so schemes that now exist across the UK.

Then as now, our starting position was that young people need both safeguards and opportunities. But our current concern is that through society misreading risk children face a myriad of restrictions that are intended to support them, whether imposed by zealous parents, by policy or by those interpreting it. We do not retreat from our advocacy of child protection but we recognise that keeping children safe conversely involves them in taking risks so that they can learn how to assess and respond to them; children will never understand risk if society prevents them from experiencing it.

Tim Gill powerfully demonstrates how opportunities for children are being constrained and provides evidence to show how measures intended to protect children can be counterproductive. Looking in detail at the issue of playgrounds, Gill points out that the rubber surfaces so long advocated in Britain as a means of reducing serious injury in playgrounds may now be the cause of more broken limbs than were sustained on hard surfaces in the past. Gill's identification of different practices in the provision of playgrounds elsewhere in Europe – which seek to challenge and empower children rather to shield them – will give hope to those who share Gill's view that a different approach is needed in the UK.

Gill argues that the concern about health and safety does not reflect the real level of risk and that the probability of adverse incidents is as important as the seriousness of their consequences. For instance, children are no more likely to be abducted or murdered by predators today than they were 30 years ago; the problem is that many parents do not know that. It will come as a surprise to many that fewer than one in ten children aged seven or eight today go to school on their own; in 1971 80 per cent did so. The average age at which children are allowed to visit a shop or a friend unaccompanied by an adult has risen by three years over the same period from seven to ten. And these restrictions on children's freedoms are not just a consequence of the growth in car use; they also reflect changes in attitude to risk in society.

Similarly, the fear of being sued, which has such a chilling effect on the providers of facilities for children, is much exaggerated. We do not have a 'compensation culture' in the UK and significant differences in the legal systems between the UK and the USA mean that we are unlikely to develop one.

Nor does Gill shrink from tackling the taboos – the exaggeration of the threat to children from strangers; the over-elaborate (and expensive) vetting system that effectively puts a third of the adult workforce under suspicion of being abusers; the sensational way the media reports tragedies involving children, which gives misleading impressions about the scale of the dangers children face. Of course, there are real dangers but the point is not just the seriousness of the consequences when things go wrong but also the likelihood of those occurring and the risks of overreacting.

There are signs of a change in culture. Gill sees hope in the sensible judgement of the Law Lords in the important test case on liability for risk which concerned a young man disabled after swimming in a public lake. The Health and Safety Executive's own campaign against petty health and safety concerns in 2006 is cited, as is recent work of the Better Regulation Commission. Despite these welcome indications, Gill believes there is much still to do.

This is a brave book and one that challenges the consensus with both evidence and passion. Gill neither belittles the risks to children nor loses sight of the need for a balanced understanding. His book is a call to all who care about children not to try to recreate a mythical age of childhood freedom and innocence but to demand realism and common sense from those who claim children's safety to be their foremost concern. The thoughts contained in the book are Tim's but the Calouste Gulbenkian Foundation hopes to promote that necessary sense of balance and proportionality in publishing his book; it is a vital contribution to a difficult but important debate.

Andrew Barnett
Director
Calouste Gulbenkian Foundation (UK)

Acknowledgements

Tim Gill would like to thank the following for help in researching and writing this book: Kate Abley, David Ball, Arthur Battram, Dea Birkett, Fraser Brown, Sue Cook, Clare Cumberlidge, Rune Elvik, Steve Farrar, Sue Gutteridge, Rick Hall, Paddy Harrop, Neil Hart, Dr Mike Hayes, Peter Heseltine, Philip Howard, Tim Hunkin, Anna Kassman-McKerrell, Jennie Lindon, Sonia Livingstone, Alison Love, Di McNeish, Hara Estroff Marano, Paul Osborne, Sue Palmer, Nigel Rogers, Susan Solomon, Mike Smith, Chris Snell, Bernard Spiegal, Liz Towner, Andy Weyman, Joe Wentworth, Rob Wheway and Helen Woolley. A special thanks to Mayer Hillman and Sandra Melville for their input and ideas over many years. Thanks also to all the British, Danish and Swedish contacts who gave their time and energy in organising visits and being interviewed.

My thanks to Calouste Gulbenkian Foundation for the opportunity to write the book, and especially to Siân Ede, Simon Richey and Felicity Luard for so capably guiding it through to publication, and for their patience and constructive feedback throughout. Finally, thanks to Kay and Rosa Watmough for their support and understanding through the process.

CHAPTER 1

Introduction

In February 2007 a primary school in Lincolnshire banned pupils from playing kiss chase and tag, because of staff concerns that playtimes were becoming too rough. The prohibition has also been seen in the US, Australia and Ireland, where in one county, half of all primary schools have banned running in the playground altogether.[1]

In April 2006, parents taking part in an online discussion on the *Times Educational Supplement* website revealed that they were seeking reassurances that the staff in hobby shops their children visited had been checked by the Criminal Records Bureau (CRB).[2] Later that year, a junior league football referee in Ashford, Kent, banned parents from taking photographs of their children, claiming that his actions were required by child protection procedures.[3]

In April 2007, two teenage girls from Bangor, Gwynedd, North Wales, were given fixed penalty notices by police officers for drawing chalk pictures on the pavement. A parent claimed that the drawings were washed away by the rain, but a police spokeswoman stated that 'chalk graffiti has been a persistent problem in upper Bangor for quite some time.'[4]

This book argues that childhood is becoming undermined by risk aversion. Activities and experiences that previous generations of children enjoyed without a second thought have been relabelled as troubling or dangerous, while the adults who still permit them are branded as irresponsible. At the extreme, as in the examples above, society appears to have become unable to cope with any adverse outcomes whatsoever, no matter how trivial or improbable. While such episodes may be rare, they fit a pattern of growing adult

Each prohibition on this sign may be defensible, however, the broader message is hard to avoid – as the graffiti addition makes clear. Photo: Tim Gill.

intervention to minimise risk at the expense of childhood experience. Adult anxieties typically focus on children's vulnerability, but they can also portray children as villains, again recasting normal childhood experiences as something more sinister.

Hugh Cunningham, Emeritus Professor of Social History at the University of Kent, wrote in his 2006 book *The Invention of Childhood* that there was one striking difference between childhood today and childhood as it has been lived for most of the last millennium:

> 'Children in the past have been assumed to have capabilities that we now rarely think they have... So fixated are we on giving our children a long and happy childhood that we downplay their abilities and their resilience.'[5]

The aim of this book is to develop Cunningham's picture: to understand how and why anxieties about risk in childhood are growing, to explore the possible consequences, and to make proposals for a more balanced approach which takes account of children's resilience. The book takes up a debate about our collective responsibility for shaping childhood, looking at the everyday risks and challenges children are likely to encounter as they grow up, especially those outside the home. It reflects the author's interests in children's play and free time as an activist and lobbyist, and more recently as a writer and commentator.

The book's main focus is on the period of childhood between the start of statutory schooling and the onset of adolescence. These crucial years – roughly between the ages of five and eleven – see many important changes in children's social and personal development, when children first start to enjoy a measure of autonomy beyond their homes. This phase generates some of the sharpest debates about freedom, protection and responsibility. Yet policymakers are typically more interested in either the early years, with the seductive promise of 'catching children young', or adolescence, by which time problems may have become manifest but the interventions available may be too little, too late.

Context: the shrinking horizons of childhood

The claim is often made that children are growing up faster today. While this may reflect children's engagement with adult culture, and their adoption of adult attitudes and behaviour, in relation to their everyday autonomy nothing could be further from the truth. For the past 30 years at least, childhood prior to adolescence has been marked by shrinking freedom of action for children, and growing adult control and supervision.

In 1971 eight out of ten children aged seven or eight years went to school on their own. By 1990 this figure had dropped to less than one in ten. Again, in 1971 the average seven-year-old was making trips to their friends or the shops on their own. By 1990 that freedom was being withheld until the age of ten, meaning that in just 19 years children had 'lost' up to three years of freedom of movement.[6] Parallel trends have been found amongst children in the US[7] and Denmark,[8] and there is little reason to doubt that the situation is similar across the developed world.

Likewise, parents today spend much more time looking after their children than previous generations. According to a 2006 report from the Future Foundation, the amount has quadrupled in just 25 years, from 25 minutes per day in 1975 to 99 minutes in 2000, and one of the reasons for this is a fear of letting children play unsupervised.[9] While the teenage and post-teenage years see a rapid expansion of young people's horizons and freedoms, this is typically in the context of a continued dependence on parents for their basic everyday needs (food, shelter, money) – a dependence that young people increasingly experience well into their twenties.

With regard to schools, the picture is more complicated. In recent years the time given for breaks has shortened dramatically. Some secondary schools have scrapped unstructured free time altogether, along with the informal play and recreational space that goes with it.[10] In the early years, the extent to which classroom practice should be play-based (and hence by definition more self-directed and child-centred) is a matter of lively debate. In primary and secondary schools, curriculum reforms have prompted a less directive approach in some subjects, though still within a framework that is tightly prescribed by the National Curriculum. However, the grip of central control appears to be loosening, in part because schools are being seen as the vehicle for delivering a range of public policy issues, from emotional literacy to parenting, citizenship and practical financial skills. The outcome of these debates remains unclear, and the growth of the extended school as a model for delivering childcare and support services muddies the waters further. Schools are certainly set to become even more significant in children's lives, but there is as yet little indication that their role will lead to any widening of childhood's horizons.

The spread of new technology is changing the very nature of childhood. Mobile phones and the internet have opened up new ways for children to engage and interact with the real world, and new virtual worlds for them to explore. Some see this as a fearful development, exposing children to novel and unmanageable threats: an issue explored in Chapter 3. Others see it as a kind of compensation for the real-world experiences enjoyed by previous generations. Children themselves, however, enjoy the freedom to communicate across the internet.

Children's immersion in online life is in part their response to parental restrictions, imposed as a result of adult fears about the threats they might otherwise encounter outside the home. While many children use the web for social contact and because it is part of their peer culture, some go online to seek out experiences that satisfy their appetite for adventure, creativity and stimulation. Indeed in some respects their media-rich bedrooms – fluid, expressive, social spaces, places of safety and security, yet also the springboards for exploration – are redolent of the dens and shelters beloved of previous generations of children.

It is a near certainty that ever more children will live more of their lives online in the future. However, it is wrong to see this as simply a compensation or substitution of one kind of space for another. The reality is that the very boundaries between these spaces are dissolving as people's work, leisure and social lives unfold in interconnected ways in the real and virtual worlds.

The changes in childhood's domain are in part a symptom of risk aversion, but they are mainly a side-effect of wider social, cultural and economic changes. The growth of road traffic and of car-dependent lifestyles, parents' longer working hours, a decline in the quantity and quality of public space, and the growth of indoor leisure activities have all reinforced the logic of containment. These changes have coincided with – and arguably helped trigger – increasingly risk averse attitudes in what sociologist Frank Furedi calls a 'culture of fear': a generalised and insidious anxiety about safety that has found expression in fears for children even though they are statistically safer than at any point in human history.[11]

2007 saw a wave of anguished debate about the behaviour of children and young people in public. This was in response to a number of highly disturbing, violent crimes involving street gangs, most notably the murder in Liverpool of 11-year-old Rhys Jones, shot in a pub car park while playing football with friends – an unwitting victim of violent gang warfare. It is clear from these events that some children and young people in a small proportion of neighbourhoods are growing up with little or no moral sense, and consequently are a real threat to those around them. Yet Home Office figures from 2006 show that only four per cent of young people had carried a knife in the previous year, and less than one per cent a gun.[12] The vast majority of children do not live in these extreme circumstances and do not share these characteristics. Their lives are marked not by chaos and moral vacuum, but by structure, supervision and control.

As the death of Rhys Jones shows with tragic clarity, some children suffer directly at the hands of their out-of-control peers. These crimes are paralleled by more diffuse deprivations arising from the fearful, anxious reactions of adults. The murder of James Bulger in 1994 illustrates how a single, devastating event can catalyse adult fears and anxieties in far-reaching ways. The tragedy led directly to the reduction in England of the age at which children can be held to know that the act they committed and were charged with was seriously wrong. This is set at ten years of age, one of the lowest baselines in Europe and a level that has generated criticism from child welfare, criminal justice and human rights agencies.[13]

In complete contrast, some groups of children, such as young carers, have to take excessive responsibility for themselves and others. Other groups, including girls and young women from certain minority ethnic communities and – especially – disabled children, may experience degrees of protection well beyond the norm. These discrepancies lead many experts in childhood to reject the idea of the 'universal child'. They argue that different children lead such different lives that all theorising has to begin with this plurality. However, childhood is a process that takes all humans from total dependence and helplessness at birth to at least a modicum of independent decision-making and autonomous existence (except in a very few cases). It is plausible to suppose that this journey has characteristics that are common to the vast majority of children. While a minority of children may not fit this pattern, this does not affect this book's core arguments and it is beyond its scope to examine them.

In a similar vein, some theorists question the possibility of substantive discussion about risk.[14] They argue that risk is a subjective phenomenon that is so influenced by social and cultural forces that reasoned debate about assessing and managing risks is not possible. Exploring these arguments is also beyond the scope of this book, which takes the more orthodox view that such a debate is both possible and necessary.

The role of risk in childhood

In making the positive case for risk in childhood, four main types of argument are offered. First, encounters with certain types of risk are said to help children learn how to manage those risks. Such arguments underpin many safety education initiatives which teach children practical skills that help them to protect themselves, such as swimming, cycling or road safety.[15]

Second, it is argued that many – perhaps most – children have an appetite for risk-taking that, if not fed somehow, will lead them to seek out situations in which they may be exposed to greater risks. For example, the development of publicly funded skate parks and other 'extreme sports' facilities is based in part on the view that children clearly want to take part in such activities, and that dedicated provision is preferable to compelling enthusiasts to pursue them in streets and other public spaces.

Third, the claim is made that children gain other benefits as a side-effect of being given the chance to undertake activities with a degree of risk. For instance, advocates for children's play assert that active outdoor play always involves some risk, but that the risks are greatly outweighed by the health and developmental benefits.[16] Similar arguments are made by those educationalists calling for a greater degree of self-directed learning opportunities, in the early years and in the school curriculum in subjects as varied as science, drama and the arts.

The last rationale in favour of risk is also a developmental one, and focuses on the longer-term benefits of risk encounters. The claim is that children build their character and personality through facing up to adverse circumstances where they know there is the possibility of injury or loss. For some advocates of this view, the predominant character traits nurtured are adventurousness and entrepreneurialism.[17] For others, they are resilience and self-reliance.[18] However, there is a common assertion that overcoming challenging situations is an essential part of living a meaningful and satisfying life.

All these arguments, if not incontestable truths about child development, have strong intuitive appeal. They are supported by evidence and authoritative opinion from psychologists and child development experts.[19] They also share two other key features. The first is that they are not unconditional pleas for the deregulation of childhood. Rather, they are calls for proportion and balance. Their force rests entirely on the circumstances: the nature of the risk, the age and developmental stage of the children under consideration and other specifics.

The second feature is that it can be difficult to assess or quantify the benefits that are being claimed. By contrast, it is comparatively easy to quantify the risks. For example, there is reliable, comprehensive data about the numbers and types of accidents and injuries that happen in children's playgrounds, as Chapter 2 will show. Data on the developmental or health benefits of playing in playgrounds, however, is harder to collect. It is often qualitative rather than quantitative and is therefore more open to methodological challenge. Statistics on the benefits of offering adventurous children challenging playgrounds rather than leaving them to explore more dangerous and uncontrolled environments, or on the long-term impact of risk experiences on children's creativity or entrepreneurialism, would be all but impossible to compile.

The upshot is that critics of risk aversion typically rely on appeals for balance, reasonableness and common sense, in the absence of the more concrete evidence base of those promoting safety or accident prevention. This asymmetry in the measurability of risks and benefits is very common in safety debates. It explains why even socially and culturally homogeneous groups of adults can disagree strongly about the most appropriate response to a given risk for a given group of children.[20] These fundamental disagreements can make it difficult to find a consensus position: so much so that one key conclusion of this book is that challenging aversion to childhood risks may sometimes require a radically different style of public policy debate.

Risk in childhood: children's behaviour and attitudes

Hugh Cunningham noted in a 2006 article to mark the publication of *The Invention of Childhood* that our ideals of a good childhood have changed little in a century. 'Children should be protected, dependent, healthy and happy,' he wrote, before concluding, 'in the last quarter of the twentieth century, many children no longer wanted to be kept in this cocoon.'[21]

In fact, children have a range of views on risk. Government consultations show that they value their safety and want adults to help them to keep safe.[22] However, market research surveys and consultation exercises consistently find a strong demand from children of all ages for greater freedom, more things to do and more places to go.[23] The wish to escape a restrictive childhood may contribute to many youth leisure choices, from pursuits like skateboarding and involvement in music subcultures to more marginal, antisocial, harmful and (at the extreme) criminal activities. What is more, some children show an appetite for adventure and excitement that persists in spite of adult anxieties. In 2002, the Child Accident Prevention Trust explored attitudes to risk and

This natural rock slide at Clifton Downs in Bristol has been used for
so long that the stone surface has been polished mirror-smooth.
Even today it draws people of all ages who seek out the chance to
test their abilities and their nerve, in spite of the obvious risks.
Photo: Tim Gill.

safety in the leisure lives of 2,000 young people, aged 11 to 14 years, from Gateshead, a relatively deprived area of north-east England. It found that about 40 per cent said they spent some of their leisure time in places they felt to be dangerous, while around half said they took part in risks and dares with their friends. Wasteland, building sites and subways or underpasses were the most popular sites, along with rivers, abandoned buildings and quarries. Young people's reasons for visiting such places spoke strongly of a search for freedom and autonomy: they included a desire to be away from adults; a search for challenge and excitement; an appetite for exploration, discovery and sometimes destruction; and a wish to have a place of their own.[24]

As they approach and pass through adolescence, children develop a good understanding of the concept of risk. Social policy researchers from Middlesex University carried out qualitative research on attitudes to risk using focus groups of children aged 11/12 and 16/17 years. They found that 'both younger and older groups had relatively sophisticated rationalisations and systems in place' for managing risk. Their research suggested that children were well-versed in how to manage such risks as road safety, sexual protection and drugs and alcohol. However, 'they appeared to be less confident in managing and negotiating social relationships that involved general teenage pressures to engage in risk activity.'[25]

What is more, there are signs that children are becoming resentful of the degree to which adults are regulating their lives in the name of safety. A story in 2006 on the Children's BBC website told how schoolchildren had started a petition after their teachers had banned the game of tag. A small minority supported the move. Alex, 13, from Sheffield, agreed with the ban 'because there's too much fall out and it is not very safe if you bump into someone'. However, most of those quoted were against it, and some put forward cogent arguments to support their stance. The views of Hannan, a teenager from Newcastle, are forthright and revealing:

> 'To be honest, adults can be very stupid at times. They ban everything, for health and safety reasons. If they're going to ban very simple stuff like this, they might as well lock all kids in empty rooms to keep them safe. Kids should be allowed to experiment and try things. Otherwise when they grow up they'll make very stupid mistakes from not getting enough experience at childhood.'[26]

Causes of risk aversion

The two usual suspects for the growth of risk aversion are the development of a compensation culture and the 'nanny state'. Of these two, the compensation culture theory appears to be a myth. Despite the emergence of 'no win no fee' arrangements and the claims management companies that generate many of them, the Law Society states that accident claims have remained fairly constant in recent years.[27] The picture is not entirely clear. Claims levels may be stable because of two trends that pull simultaneously in opposite directions: claims being made for incidents that historically would not have prompted legal action, and agencies adopting more defensive practices for fear of being sued. Whatever the reality of the claims culture, the widespread fear of litigation reinforces the belief that all adverse outcomes are blameworthy. It thus fosters risk aversion even if it is not a primary cause, and encourages the spread of bureaucratic approaches to risk management.

The nanny state contention has a stronger case to answer. In recent years regulatory bureaucracies like the Health and Safety Executive (HSE) and Ofsted have grown in size and reach. The typical approach of these agencies, which relies heavily on prescribed procedures, can limit the scope for flexibility and professional judgement. The HSE in particular arguably struggles to accept that encountering risks can be intrinsically beneficial.[28] Beyond these regulatory bodies, the spread of state bureaucratic influence, especially in the form of centrally determined targets for public services, can also undermine professional judgement. It may skew services to deliver outcomes that are more easily measured (such as accident reduction, educational qualifications or arrests of young offenders) and to ignore those outcomes that are harder to measure. However, when it comes to children it is anachronistic to place the primary responsibility for risk aversion in the lap of the nanny state. As is argued in Chapter 2, confusion about child safety predates the expansion of the HSE and Ofsted, or the spread of a culture of centrally determined targets.

Legal and public policy context

Coverage of health and safety debates in the popular media can paint a picture of the relentless spread of excessive risk aversion. In fact, a more thoughtful approach to risk is beginning to emerge in public policy. Perhaps the clearest demonstration of this comes from the work of the Better Regulation Commission, but it can also be seen in recent pronouncements from the HSE, and also in a landmark legal ruling from the House of Lords.

The Better Regulation Commission is a government-appointed body charged with improving the Government's approach to regulation, especially in business. The Commission's first report, *Risk, Responsibility and Regulation: Whose risk is it anyway?* was categorical in stating that 'we all share a responsibility for managing risk and ... within the right circumstances, risk can be beneficial and should be encouraged.'[29] It has placed centre stage questions about the ways that responsibility for managing risks is shared between individuals, agencies and the state.

Picking up the theme, in August 2006 the HSE launched a campaign with the strapline 'Get a Life' that was highly critical of petty health and safety concerns. The campaign declared that sensible risk management was not about creating a totally risk-free society. Rather it was (to quote the HSE website) about 'balancing benefits and risks, with a focus on reducing real risks – both those which arise more often and those with serious consequences.'[30] The HSE initiative argued convincingly that some so-called 'health and safety' stories were myths or distortions, while others were convenient excuses to justify unpopular decisions or cover up management failures. However it also accepted that sometimes those charged with ensuring safety were guilty of concentrating effort on trivial risks and of generating unnecessary paperwork.

Relevant legislation also shows a common-sense approach to assigning responsibility for managing risks. For instance, the Health and Safety at Work Act 1974 calls for risks in workplaces to be kept 'as low as reasonably practicable'. Both the Act itself and subsequent regulations and interpretations make it clear that the benchmark of 'reasonable practicability' does not require the elimination of all possible risk. Likewise the Occupier's Liability Act 1957 requires occupiers to take 'such care as in all the circumstances of the case is reasonable'.

With regard to the courts and case law, there is no evidence that judges are systematically making judgements that fuel risk aversion or run counter to common-sense intuitions about where the blame should lie. A Law Lords ruling in 2004 illustrates this well. The case involved a liability claim arising from a permanently disabling injury that John Tomlinson, then aged 18, sustained after going swimming in a lake in a country park managed by Congleton Borough Council. The case hinged on the Council's duty of care, and whether or not it extended to taking steps to manage the risks highlighted by this tragic event. Tomlinson's claim was rejected, overturning the decision of the Court of Appeal. Lord Scott stated that 'of course there is some risk of accidents arising from the joie de vivre of the young. But that is no reason for imposing a grey and dull safety regime on everyone.' Fellow presiding judge Lord Hoffmann expanded on the reasoning behind the judgement:

> 'The question of what amounts to [reasonable care] depends upon assessing ... not only the likelihood that someone may be injured and the seriousness of the injury which may occur, but also the social value of the activity which gives rise to the risk and the cost of preventative measures. These factors have to be balanced against each other ... and may lead to the conclusion that even though injury is foreseeable ... it is still in all the circumstances reasonable to do nothing about it.' [31]

There is little to justify calls for a fundamental change in liability law. The Compensation Act 2006 implicitly recognised this, since it merely emphasised the legal status quo about the need for the courts to take a balanced approach to risks and benefits. However, there remain public policy concerns about the ways that risk management is understood and undertaken. The recent pronouncements of the Better Regulation Commission and the HSE are positive signs and provide a helpful context for taking the issues forward. Some of their analyses – about the importance of good evidence, the pitfalls of emotive responses to tragedy, the need to be alert to vested interests and the potential side-effects of quick fixes – are developed later in this book.

Elsewhere debate is growing about children and risk. In 2006 the Royal Society for the Encouragement of Arts, Manufactures and Commerce (RSA) set up a Risk Commission, with childhood a major theme.[32] In September of the same year one of Britain's largest children's charities, the Children's Society, announced a two-year Good Childhood Inquiry. The launch highlighted contradictory views about, on the one hand, the risks faced by children and, on the other, the threats children pose to society.[33] This book's aim is to contribute to these and other initiatives, in part by exploring how the debate changes when it is children, not adults, who are the focus of the risks in question.

The book's focus

This book considers a small number of contested issues as case studies in order to bring out some key themes and arguments. The first and most thoroughly explored topic is playground safety. This case study is followed by briefer examinations of antisocial behaviour, bullying, child protection, fear of strangers and online risks.

The geographical focus is on children in the UK, though with a limited look at a small number of other developed nations to broaden the perspective. These international comparisons strongly suggest that risk aversion is greater in the UK than in some comparable European countries. In the Netherlands, Germany, Denmark and Sweden, for example, citizens and institutions appear to be more able to resist the forces that fuel risk aversion. By contrast, risk aversion appears to be even more acute in the USA than in the UK. In America, the compensation culture is a reality, and a major cause of risk aversion. Fear of liability is grounded not just in misperception or misinformation, but in fundamental differences in the way the legal system handles litigation. Lord Hoffmann, one of the UK's leading law lords, has highlighted how British personal liability law differs from its American counterpart. US liability cases are conducted in front of juries, and may involve class action and punitive damages, all of which raise the stakes for defendants. In the UK, the risks to defendants are lower because tariffs are used for setting compensation levels, and the losing side may have to pay the costs of the victor.[34]

Looking further afield at children living in poor and developing countries, it is clear that the risks they face are qualitatively different and more severe than those encountered by children in affluent, industrialised nations. Absolute poverty, shortages of food and water, disease, military conflict and inadequate public services threaten the very lives of many millions of children across the world, but to explore these risks is beyond the scope of this book.

CHAPTER 2

Playgrounds

The public playground provides a case study for looking at the influence of risk aversion on children's everyday lives. Playgrounds are familiar places, both in adult memories of childhood and in villages, towns and cities today. Helpfully for this book, they have also been the subject of an enormous amount of research into safety over the last 30 years, and the focus of lively and constructive debate. Playgrounds bring together the interested parties represented in public policy discussions about children and risk. Providers, managers, regulators, safety agencies, legislators, insurers, lawyers, the media, parents and children themselves all have a stake in what goes on in the playground. Chapter 2 explores this example of childhood risk, showing how all these interests interact and influence children's experiences.

A brief history of playground safety

Public playgrounds have been around for perhaps only a hundred years. They were promoted by nineteenth-century social reformers as a solution to concerns about children's socialisation, health and fitness.[35] Early playgrounds were supervised, but cost considerations meant that, as they increased in number, supervision gradually became less common. By the Second World War, across the developed world, playgrounds were an established and widespread response to social problems associated with health, urbanisation and immigration.

The physical design of playgrounds changed little until the 1960s, and until then the question of safety was not much considered. Indeed some of the most popular items of equipment such as the plank swing and 'witches hat' (a suspended circular seat-platform that rocked and span around a central column) caused levels of injury, and even deaths, that would be unacceptable today.[36]

In the 1970s concern about playground safety, prompted in part by a number of tragic accidents, led the British Standards Institute to produce a set of safety standards. While not a legal requirement, these provided guidance (endorsed by government) about the design, installation and upkeep of playgrounds. Other agencies took up the issue, including the National Playing Fields Association, the Royal Society for the Prevention of Accidents and the campaigning group Fair Play for Children. Among the changes being called for was the introduction of impact absorbing surfacing under equipment, to reduce the risk of severe head injuries caused by children falling from a height.[37]

This move eventually came to the notice of consumer groups. In 1988 the Consumers Association published a report into playground safety that raised concerns about design, maintenance and access and included a call for greater use of safety surfacing. Around the same time the issue was taken up by the BBC TV consumer programme *That's Life*, in what was arguably the apex of campaigning activity on playground safety.

For much of its 21-year run (1973–94), *That's Life* was a national institution. It is one of the few TV programmes that could claim to have shaped public policy. For example, Childline – the national telephone helpline for children – has its origins in *That's Life*. One focus of its playground safety campaign was impact absorbing surfacing. In an episode broadcast in May 1990, the presenters explained that an MP had started his own campaign to make safety surfacing a legal requirement in all playgrounds,[38] and prominent coverage was given of the case of an eight-year-old girl who died after falling off a swing and hitting her head on the tarmac below.

The episode gave the impression that playgrounds were dangerous places, that the main source of danger was hard surfaces, and that any injury, no matter how serious or slight, was a sign of failure on the part of providers. Figures were given about accidents reported by viewers, but these gave no indication of the prevalence of injuries and made no meaningful comparisons with other activities.

In fact, playgrounds are by any standard comparatively safe environments for children, and have been for some decades and certainly were at the time of the *That's Life* campaign. David Ball, Professor of Risk Management at Middlesex University and one of the world's leading experts on playground safety, systematically researched playground injuries in both 1988 and 2002. He found comparatively low levels of injuries, especially serious ones. In 2002, Ball estimated that, each year, perhaps half a million injuries and around 21,000 visits to hospital accident and emergency services occur as a result of equipment-related accidents in public playgrounds.[39] Only a minority of these involve falls from equipment. While the figures may seem large, the odds of a child sustaining a playground injury are about one in 16 per year, while the odds of visiting A&E are around one in 200. So in a typical primary school population, perhaps one or two children a year will visit A&E after an accident involving equipment in public playgrounds. Ball estimates that activities like swimming and soccer are many times more dangerous.[40] Moreover, playground accident rates have been steady for years with little or no evidence of a decline, in spite of the periodic introduction of new equipment standards and the spread of impact absorbing surfacing and other safety measures.

The chances of a child being killed as the result of an accident involving playground equipment are vanishingly low. David Ball's research looked at fatalities as well as injuries and, as with many other types of accident, the data takes the shape of an 'accident pyramid', with large numbers of minor injuries, smaller numbers of more serious ones and an extremely small number of life-threatening injuries or fatalities. In a 13-year period, Ball found that perhaps three or four children had died as a result of equipment-related injuries, including falls: around one child fatality every three or four years. Again, the figures have been at this level for decades. This means that, each year,

Swingset in a playground in Central Park, New York City. The all-embracing seats, safety surfacing and fencing are symptomatic of adult anxiety about children's safety. Photo: Nils Norman.

the odds of a child dying from such a playground accident are less than 30 million to one.[41] Ball's conclusion is that:

> 'Playground risk is extremely small in terms of fatalities, and in terms of lesser
> injuries far lower than for most traditional sports which children are encouraged
> to engage in, and in any case about the same as the risk encountered at home.'[42]

Needless to say, such an assessment is of little comfort if you are the parent of that one child in 30 million. However, it is the task of policymakers to make judgements based on evidence and arguments in the round, and not just on the basis of emotional responses or on what victims believe might have helped. The Better Regulation Commission's 2006 report *Risk, Responsibility and Regulation* captured the public policy implications of simplistic reactions to extreme events:

> 'Misfortune, tragedy and loss sit at the heart of many risk debates and
> government can be overwhelmed by the need to respond sympathetically and
> try to make things better. This frequently clouds the process of choosing the
> best response and can make the option of "no action" appear both uncaring and
> irresponsible.'[43]

In place of confused responses, the report calls for considered debate that moves beyond the immediate reactions of grief, guilt, and anger, and that separates fact from emotion. This is crucial, because the plea to adopt the point of view of the victims or the bereaved cannot help but lead to excessively risk averse responses to tragedy. Such a plea is quite different from an appeal for sympathy. It is a request that we adopt the bereaved's inevitably revised value system. If we were always required to see the world through the eyes of the most unlucky, then we would always choose zero risk.

Safety surfacing remains a primary focus of playground safety efforts. This is in spite of a growing body of research that suggests that its effectiveness in reducing accidents is questionable. It was only ever intended to protect against head impacts resulting from falls from significant heights onto hard ground. Such events are among the most severe and life-threatening types of playground accident, but also among the rarest. Ball has shown that in a best-case scenario, safety surfacing might result in 'up to 0.2 fatalities per annum *potentially* being saved'.[44] He conducted a review of published research on the effectiveness of surfacing, and found mixed results:

'Some studies find benefits of some surface types in terms of reduced injury risk and others do not. Overall ... it is perhaps fairest to conclude from what is now known that compliant surfaces may have some beneficial effect under certain conditions.'[45]

The strongest argument against safety surfacing is that, on cost-benefit grounds, it is a highly disproportionate response to a minimal risk, given the extreme rarity of the injuries it is intended to prevent. If it is justified as a safety measure, then clearly it should be fitted in all playgrounds, and that is indeed largely the case. The rubber surfacing most commonly used costs up to 40 per cent of the total capital cost of a playground.[46] This means that, over the decade or so following the *That's Life* playground safety campaign, perhaps £200 to £300 million has been spent on a measure that, on the most optimistic assumptions, would have saved the lives of one or two children.[47] The same period saw perhaps 1,300 child pedestrians killed and around 40,000 seriously injured, most in streets close to their homes. Cost-benefit analyses show that residential traffic calming is at least ten times as effective in reducing accident numbers as playground safety surfacing. Moreover, unlike surfacing, it has a proven effect on reducing casualty rates in real-life situations. So the same sum would beyond doubt have saved far more lives if it had been invested in streets rather than playgrounds.[48] Simply providing more playgrounds may have saved more lives, since it would have reduced children's travel distances and hence the likelihood of their being run over.[49]

The argument against safety surfacing is strengthened by the evident side-effects of its roll-out across the country. The demand for this safety measure undoubtedly led cash-strapped local authorities to shift their spending priorities. In 1995, Peter Heseltine, former head of playground safety at the Royal Society for the Prevention of Accidents (RoSPA), offered the blunt conclusion that:

'In the UK the cost of surfacing has resulted in equipment being removed, playgrounds closed and only small amounts of items purchased for new playgrounds – and all without much evidence that it is effective in reducing any accidents other than the extremely rare direct head fall.'[50]

Evidence is emerging of other side-effects of impact absorbing surfacing. A growing number of experts think that the rubber safety surfacing most often used in the UK may lead to *more* broken arms than other types of surface.[51] This may be a biomechanical effect caused by the way that long bones behave when children hold out their arms and fall onto a rubber surface. However, it may also be an example of what risk experts call 'risk compensation'. Risk compensation occurs when a person responds to a safety measure by taking greater risks. For instance, a mountain climber equipped with ropes, harness and helmet will tackle peaks that an unequipped scrambler would never attempt. To take a more everyday scenario, the reason why the introduction of antilock brake systems in cars failed to reduce traffic accident rates was because drivers simply adapted their behaviour by driving faster, tailgating more closely and braking later.[52] The hypothesis is that some children playing in playgrounds with safety surfacing will be less careful on equipment because they think they will be safe if they fall, while for the same reason their parents may pay less attention to what their children are doing. Such behavioural effects are common, and are beginning to be the focus of systematic research; for instance, one study has suggested that children who wear cycle helmets may alter their behaviour.[53] However, the impact of risk compensation on accidents and other outcomes can be hard to measure. If it is happening in playgrounds it will undermine the benefits of special surfacing. Risk compensation is particularly relevant when the risks being addressed are – as in playgrounds – statistically very rare. As David Ball notes, there is always 'the possibility that interventions will create new risks of their own which, especially if the target risk is small, could result in more harm, not less.'[54]

Safety surfacing is not the only manifestation of excessive aversion to risk in the playground. For decades, almost every aspect of playground design and management has been specified in great detail, largely on the grounds of safety. The European safety standards for playgrounds, drawn up by the European Committee for Standardization, CEN, with input from national standards bodies such as the British Standards Institute, run to eight volumes, with four more to come.[55] RoSPA recommends visual inspections on a weekly or even daily basis.[56] The National Playing Fields Association's 'six acre standard' – the only national guidance on creating play areas in new housing developments – specifies the numbers of pieces of equipment that playgrounds of different sizes should contain. It also states that all play areas should be surrounded by dog-proof fencing, and proposes that all sites should include 'buffer areas' to reduce the impact of children playing on others who live nearby.[57]

None of this guidance is a legal requirement. It is merely a statement of what the relevant agency considers to be good practice. Some of it may be highly speculative.

However, most providers treat much or all of it as mandatory, fearing the consequences of non-compliance. Insurance providers often make compliance with safety standards and guidance a condition of insurance, regardless of their legal or scientific status or their relevance to local needs or circumstances. Liability claims are made – and sometimes conceded – on the basis of non-compliance, even if there is little or no causal connection with the injury. Yet as David Ball notes, an over-reliance on standards and guidance creates problems of its own:

> 'Most standards offer sound advice, but over-attention to *minutely detailed* measurements can in some circumstances be misleading and inappropriate. A general problem with prescribed safety criteria is that they encourage a less thoughtful approach to risk management. If a duty holder believes that by following a certain specification to the letter, safety will have been achieved, then s/he is less likely to engage in *goal-seeking* initiatives to manage risk.' [58]

As was the case with the introduction of safety surfacing, so, too, the uncritical application of standards has diminished the quality and number of playgrounds. Rob Wheway, an experienced play consultant and researcher who advises the Child Accident Prevention Trust on the issue, describes how two local authorities removed newly installed swings throughout their areas after learning that they marginally failed one aspect of the relevant standard. In his view, 'there was no reason to believe that this minor technical failure created any additional risk.'[59]

In the US, playground safety is if anything a greater preoccupation than in the UK, even though accident rates are comparable – doubtless a reflection of the enormous influence of the fear of litigation.[60] Joe Frost is Professor Emeritus in Education at the University of Texas and has an interest in play. He describes how, in 2003, regulations in Texas led to the prohibition of 11 types of equipment from child-care facilities, homes and agencies, including fulcrum seesaws, overhead rings, parallel bars and vertical slide poles. His concerns are echoed by the US lawyer and writer Philip Howard, founder of the not-for-profit organisation Common Good, which campaigns for legal reforms to curb the spread and impact of litigation. Howard also describes examples of overcautious approaches to playground safety, including in the town of Bristol, Connecticut, where all seesaws and merry-go-rounds were removed from playgrounds.[61]

By contrast, playground safety appears to prompt less concern in some other

European countries. Playground equipment standards have been adopted across Europe. As in the UK, they have the status of good practice guidance and are not a legal requirement (except in Germany). Yet UK playground designers who visit Germany, Denmark, the Netherlands and Sweden agree that playgrounds typically look less sterile and safety-obsessed than at home.[62] For instance, these playgrounds rarely feature the expensive rubber safety surfacing most commonly used in the UK and US. Three case studies illustrate the point.

In 1996, the authorities in Malmö, the third largest city in Sweden, began a major programme of park and playground redevelopment. In 2006, I interviewed Sten Göransson and Camilla Anderson from the municipality's parks department about its approach to playground safety. They took the view that safety is just one of a number of factors that should be considered when planning playgrounds, and that accidents are to be expected from time to time. They told me:

> 'We follow the European standards and check all playgrounds once a week. The municipality is responsible for keeping all play equipment in good shape. Although we can't avoid accidents, where there is a problem that we have known about but not done anything about then the municipality is responsible. But if somebody falls and breaks an arm that is just something that happens. Of course it worries us but there is always a risk when you play and move your body.... You are there at your own risk.'

Since the early 1990s, the German city of Freiburg has been installing public playgrounds that make extensive use of slopes, logs, boulders, plants, sand and other natural features. The resulting spaces can look more like overgrown bombsites than traditional playgrounds. In 2005, I met the Deputy Director of Parks, Harald Rabhein, and asked him about playground safety in these more naturalistic places. He replied:

> 'Clearly there are more hazards, and they are more varied, in natural play spaces compared to traditional play areas. In general children learn to take more care

---

OPPOSITE: **In staffed adventure playgrounds like this one in Tokyo, Japan, children are given free rein to try out risky, challenging activities. They learn for themselves how to avoid injury. Photo: Nils Norman.**

**While most British adventure playgrounds feature semi-permanent timber
structures, this Japanese playground adopts a more free-form approach.
It captures something of the original inspiration for adventure playgrounds:
children's self-built constructions on post-war bombsites. Photo: Nils Norman.**

and responsibility for their safety in the nature play spaces and as a result accident rates have not increased.'[63]

The Danish landscape architect Helle Nebelong has designed some award-winning public play spaces in Copenhagen that, like those in Freiburg, are inspired by natural, wild environments. She rejects standardisation in the firmest of terms, arguing that in fact it can create its own dangers. In her view:

> 'When the distance between all the rungs in a climbing net or a ladder is exactly the same, the child has no need to concentrate on where he puts his feet. Standardisation is dangerous because play becomes simplified and the child does not have to worry about his movements. This lesson cannot be carried over to all the knobbly and asymmetrical forms with which one is confronted throughout life.'[64]

Recent developments in playground safety

In recent years attitudes towards playground safety have relaxed. Advocates for children's play had become increasingly frustrated by what they saw as a preoccupation with safety at all costs, a view echoed by some providers and playground equipment manufacturers. The issue was taken up at the national level by the Play Safety Forum (PSF). This government-sponsored body includes representatives from most of the key interest groups, including the HSE, other leading safety and accident prevention agencies, professional associations, local government and insurance representatives as well as advocacy groups and industry experts. It had historically taken a technical, standards-based approach to playground safety, mirroring the philosophy of other industries.

The PSF began to rethink its position on safety in 2001. First, it explored some basic questions about the role and purpose of play provision, reaffirming that playgrounds existed first and foremost for children's enjoyment and benefit. It also looked at the evidence on playground accidents and injuries, a task made easier by David Ball's research into this topic on behalf of the HSE, which the PSF was able to refer to. In 2002, the PSF published *Managing Risk in Play Provision*, a statement that recognised the importance and benefits of providing children with opportunities for taking risks.[65] Its key message was that playground providers should 'strike a balance between the risks and the benefits'. It stated that accidents and injuries were 'a universal part of childhood' that had 'a positive role in child development', and that children had 'a range of competences and abilities, including a growing ability to assess and manage risk'. It accepted the possibility of tragedy, saying that it may be unavoidable that play provision 'exposes children to the risk – the very low risk – of serious injury or even death'. Finally, it rejected the view that safety was an overriding objective that trumped all others, stating that designers need to make compromises between competing goals, and that these were 'a matter of judgement, not of mechanistic assessment'.

The arguments put forward in the PSF statement are now largely accepted. Its legal basis has been affirmed by the organisation Playlink, which in 2006 commissioned the law firm Public Interest Lawyers to give an authoritative view of its legal soundness. The resulting counsel's opinion stated that a value-based policy that is grounded in the PSF statement does meet legal and regulatory requirements about reasonableness.[66]

The PSF statement has helped to create a climate in which providers can build less safety-oriented, more challenging playgrounds. For instance Stirling Council in Scotland has in the last few years opened a number of playgrounds inspired by ideas from Scandinavia and Germany, and the community regeneration charity Groundwork UK has been championing a similar approach.

The statement has also influenced safety policy debates in other sectors. In 2005, the Institute of Sports and Recreation Management, one of the members of the Play Safety Forum, rejected calls for children to have one-to-one adult supervision in public swimming pools, even though such guidance was intended to lower the chances of a child drowning. It did so in part because it argued that this might mean fewer children getting the chance to learn to swim in the relatively safe environment of a pool, and therefore more children and adults unable to swim and so potentially at risk of drowning.[67]

The statement has even influenced the setting of safety standards. In 2006, following representations from UK delegates, European playground safety experts proposed to relax their standard on the need for safety surfacing underneath playground equipment.[68] Such a move is, according to David Ball, highly unusual in the safety standards industry.[69]

Conclusions

The playground safety initiatives of the 1970s and 1980s, of which the *That's Life* campaign was perhaps the most well-known example, were not without merit. Some genuinely dangerous equipment was removed from public playgrounds, and some reckless or negligent manufacturers were forced to raise their standards or go out of business. Playground providers doubtless took safety more seriously and improved their systems. However, these initiatives also led to a preoccupation with safety across the industry, almost to the exclusion of other goals. With the benefit of hindsight, they also revealed some of the key characteristics of excessive risk aversion.

First, they reinforced the idea that playgrounds should be free of risk, and that any accidents or injuries were a sign of failure. This view was expressed by a parent interviewed on *That's Life*. Commenting on why her local playground was so much better now that it had been fitted with rubber safety surfacing, she remarked: 'before, the surface was quite hard ... but now, they can jump around, they can fall, and it won't hurt them at all. They love it.' This view of risk may in part have been the result of the inappropriate transfer to playgrounds of principles from workplace health and safety. As the PSF statement notes, in most workplaces the presence of physical risks – vertical drops, wobbly bridges or narrow balance beams – is a problem to be solved, whereas in a playground it is often an asset.

Second, much of the campaigning and awareness-raising placed tragedy centre stage. The occurrence of even a single episode of catastrophic loss was enough to justify a demand for preventative action. The notion that such events might sometimes be down to bad luck, or that preventative action might be impractical or dispropor-tionate, was resisted.

Third, there was little or no attempt to look systematically at accident data or to place playground accidents in a wider context. Even in the 1970s, the problem was not that there was a lack of data, but that it was either ignored or misinterpreted in order to fit the conventional wisdom.[70] This omission is especially striking given the much greater risk of injury elsewhere, most obviously from traffic accidents in residential streets.

The fourth risk averse characteristic was the degree of faith placed in the safety expert's quick fix – in this case, the technical fixes provided by standards and safety surfacing. The point is not that standards are of no use, or that safety surfacing has no benefit, but that the advantages of rigid compliance with technical standards were overemphasised, while the drawbacks were not fully examined. This in turn led providers to place an excessive focus on technical interventions, at the expense of other responses that might have been more cost-effective, such as appropriate maintenance and inspection regimes.

The fifth and most fundamental characteristic revealed by these playground safety initiatives was that they implicitly embraced what might be called a 'deficit model' of childhood: the view that children were essentially vulnerable. *That's Life* took this view to extremes: the episode described earlier in the chapter featured a demonstration of the benefits of safety surfacing that involved dropping china plates onto, first, the studio floor and, second, some rubber matting – with predictable results. The implicit assumption was that children were fragile, incompetent, accident-prone, unable to deal with adversity and incapable of learning how to look after themselves or to manage their own safety. Therefore, the adult role was to safeguard children from their own shortcomings and from the perceived dangers of the wider world, rather than to help them face those dangers and learn how to overcome them.

The final insight gained from looking at the playground safety initiatives of the 1970s and 80s is that they predate both the rise of a compensation culture and the nanny state. Both of these two alleged ills may well have a role in fuelling the spread of excessive aversion to risk in children's playgrounds. However, its primary source is different, and has to do with deeply held and rarely questioned values and beliefs about children's competences.

CHAPTER 3

The spread of risk averse attitudes to childhood

This chapter explores some other domains of childhood where risk aversion is in evidence: antisocial behaviour, bullying, child protection and vetting, fear of strangers and online risks. These topics have been chosen because they exemplify some key facets of the wider debate and highlight some important public policy issues. They also reflect the book's focus on children between the ages of about five and eleven years, and on risks associated with the everyday lives of the majority of children in the UK.

Antisocial behaviour

In Halesowen in July 2006 the police arrested and DNA tested three 12-year-olds for climbing a cherry tree on public land. None of the children had ever been in trouble with the police before. The West Midlands Police were unapologetic in the face of complaints from parents, saying that such incidents of antisocial behaviour were 'robustly' dealt with and explaining that 'by targeting what may seem relatively low-level crime we aim to prevent it developing into more serious matters.'[71]

In April the same year, the Willow Park Housing Trust in Manchester wrote a letter to Michelle Mann about her son Ben. The Trust stated that 'Willow Park has received a complaint about antisocial behaviour perpetrated by your son Ben and his friends, who have been playing football and causing a disturbance,' and that 'it takes all complaints seriously.' Clearly it does, because Ben Mann, the cause of the disturbance and the perpetrator of the act, was just three years old.[72]

Antisocial behaviour and worse by children is not a trivial matter. In many communities it is severe and causes genuine anguish. The victims include other children, both directly at the hands of perpetrators, and indirectly through restrictions imposed by parents fearful of letting their children out. Tackling it requires a range of interventions, including legal sanctions. Nonetheless the episodes described above, while arguably rare, are evidence of a growing overreaction to minor problems. Adult hostility to low-level misbehaviour by children – noise, scratched cars, broken windows, trampled flower beds – is nothing new. What is new is the trend for the police and other public services to impose formal sanctions for petty offences. Rod Morgan, former chair of the Youth Justice Board, was concerned enough to have said in 2006 that 'too many children are being criminalised for behaviour that could be dealt with informally by ticking them off and speaking to their parents.'[73]

Even the police are troubled about this form of risk aversion. In 2004, Paul Scott-Lee, Chief Constable of West Midlands Police, stated in a newspaper report that his

---

OPPOSITE: The author's daughter climbing a tree in Golder's Hill Park, London. In some neighbourhoods such behaviour is deemed sufficiently troubling to warrant official intervention. Photo: Tim Gill.

force receives about three million non-emergency calls a year, and that the majority are what the police would initially call complaints about antisocial behaviour. He continued:

> 'The interesting thing to me is when you ask them what they are worried about, it's not young people committing crime or young people committing criminal damage ... it is actually young people just being there. Young people simply existing is now a major source of concern for people.'[74]

The phenomenon of play fighting provides a revealing case study of changing adult attitudes to young children's behaviour. Mock-aggressive play is part of the natural behaviour of the young of many if not all higher mammals.[75] Most boys (and some girls) engage in various kinds of rough-and-tumble play, play fighting and combative role play, whether in streets, the local park, the school playground or the back garden. The sight of children engaged in apparently aggressive play can be troubling. Nonetheless 20 years ago, many adults who became aware of children play fighting would probably have turned a blind eye. Today, such games are banned from most nurseries and many schools, and are often a source of embarrassment or anxiety for parents whose children are seen playing them in public.

However, in her book *We Don't Play With Guns Here*, early-years researcher Penny Holland argues that for younger children play fighting, gun play and rough-and-tumble play are neither atavistic displays of animal aggression nor mindless re-enactments of yesterday's TV.[76] Rather, they are outward signs of a sophisticated and largely unconscious learning process. According to psychologists, these forms of play allow children to perfect some important social skills in a context where real harm is not part of the game. For instance, they give children invaluable experience in reading facial expressions and body language and they enable children to learn about their position and status in their peer group.[77] What is more, researchers have known for years that most children quickly become skilled at reading the body language of play fighting – unlike adults, who can find it difficult to distinguish between play and the real thing.[78]

Two linked anxieties lie behind adult reactions to play fighting: fear of being blamed if any children are hurt or upset, and a sense that allowing such play is somehow bad practice. As a result, play fighting has come to be seen as a disturbing facet of childhood, and one from which children need to be saved. The ironic outcome is that young boys, in particular, are deprived of experiences that may well help them negotiate tricky social situations better, and hence keep themselves safer, as they grow up. Another side-effect of the bans, as Holland notes, is that adults often demonise the behaviour and label those boys who engage in it as unruly troublemakers: a prophecy that some then go on to fulfil.

It is crucial though not always easy to distinguish between – on the one hand – play fighting and other low-level skirmishes amongst children, or between children and adults and – on the other – more serious thoughtless or deliberate antisocial acts. The former are, like minor accidents, formative childhood experiences; they do not presage a life of crime or antisocial behaviour. They help children to understand the norms and conventions that shape much of social activity. This system of rules, which could be called an everyday morality, comes into play when deciding, among other things: whether or not to help someone we do not know; how to respond to a joke at our expense; when to stand up for ourselves and argue with someone we disagree with, and when it is better to back off; how to deal with the abuse of power; how far loyalty can justify actions that might harm those outside our circle; how to respond to, and where appropriate resist, peer pressure; whom we can trust and how far we can trust them.

Mastering everyday codes of behaviour is no mean feat. It is partly learnt through the guidance of parents and other significant adults in children's lives, and by witnessing adults' behaviour. But children also learn from their peers and from their own experience: from being active participants in social interactions and appreciating the consequences of these interactions.

A more balanced public policy response to concerns about children's misbehaviour would not mean ignoring the problem altogether. However, it would mean encouraging more proportionate measures that acknowledge the importance for children of self-directed experience, and that accept they will sometimes make mistakes but will learn from these.

Such a position would encourage and support people and communities to try to resolve their own differences before involving official bodies. This is not an easy matter, since it depends upon the existence of a degree of trust and mutual respect between people of all ages – commodities which often seem to be in short supply. Research conducted by the Institute for Public Policy Research (IPPR) suggests that adults in the UK are less willing than those in other European countries to step in and address low-level public misbehaviour by teenagers.[79] Nonetheless the prospects for improvement are poor if disproportionate responses to such incidents deprive children of the experiences that enable them to learn how to interact with people around them.

Bullying

'Dad, those boys were bullying us.' The words came from my daughter, pointing to three boys, all younger than herself, none of whom she had ever met before. We were in a local park with a friend of hers. 'What were they doing?' I asked. She explained that the boys had started teasing her and her friend during a treasure hunt. She was soon off playing again, but although the incident itself was trivial, there was something significant in my daughter's choice of the word 'bullying' to describe the boys' actions.

Bullying is a serious problem. A 2007 report from the House of Commons Education Select Committee claimed that around a third of all young adults were bullied at some point in their childhoods. The growth in use of mobile phones and social networking websites is opening up new contexts in which bullying can take place. Case studies show that victims' lives can be destroyed by brutal, sustained abuse from peers. However, some anti-bullying initiatives are beginning to show signs of excessive risk aversion in the way that they define the problem.

Experts used to agree that bullying involved sustained, repeated maltreatment based on a power imbalance between victim and perpetrator. They distinguished this type of damaging behaviour from less serious conflicts and disagreements. The psychologist Valerie Besag discussed playground behaviour in her contribution to *Bullying: A practical guide to coping for schools*, published in 2002, stating:

> 'There is a place for some degree of teasing, challenging and critical comment in
> the normal interactions of childhood play... It is possible to become over-
> protective of young people. They need to be able to meet challenges and
> justifiable criticism to prepare them for the teasing, taunting and the range of
> other challenges they will undoubtedly meet later in life... Over-involvement and

direction by adults may thwart the emerging skills of decision-making, imaginative play and creativity... The role of adults in the playground is to be vigilant and supportive, ready to step in, but only where necessary.'[80]

However, more recently this distinction has been blurred by an apparent broadening of the definition. In a 2006 hearing of the House of Commons Education Select Committee, Michele Elliott, Chief Executive Officer of Kidscape – one of the UK's leading child safety charities – defined bullying as 'a sustained, deliberate attack on somebody with the intention of causing pain, and that could be verbal, physical, sexual, racial, whatever you want to call it; it is all bullying when it is deliberate. Teasing is very easy to describe. I can tease you and you can tease me and, if we are enjoying it, that is great. If it is causing pain, then that is bullying.' Recent peer-reviewed research on the subject has taken a similar position, defining bullying as 'any form of victimisation or harassment perpetrated by another child or young person'.[81]

It may be difficult for adults to judge whether or not a particular incident is bullying, and to decide how best to intervene. However, simply redefining all deliberately unpleasant behaviour as bullying does not solve this problem, it merely brushes it under the carpet. The unintended side-effect of such redefinition is that adults are likely to feel under growing pressure to step in whenever children fall out or argue with each other, causing confusion in the minds of children, parents and school staff. In an atmosphere of heightened media and public awareness of the problem, there is a real danger that adults will overreact and suppress behaviour that, unlike bullying, has a key role in helping children to learn for themselves how to deal with difficult social situations.

Anti-bullying agencies may argue that many schools are still failing to give enough attention to the issue, so to complain about an overreaction is unhelpful. This misses the point. Tackling bullying is a risk management problem *par excellence*, and an explicitly balanced approach is needed from the outset. Blurring the distinction between bullying and less serious conflicts hinders rather than helps this. School playgrounds give many children their only opportunity to socialise and spend time with their friends and peers face to face in a relatively adult-free space. So getting the distinction right between bullying and everyday unpleasantness is more important then ever.

Child protection, vetting and contact between children and adults

The Central Herts YMCA runs a range of classes for the local community, including courses for older people on computers and the internet. A local school suggested the idea of getting teenagers in to help as volunteers on these courses, exploiting their greater expertise in the subject while at the same time fostering some positive interactions between two age groups that rarely find common ground. However, a problem emerged because they were minors. Child protection procedures meant that all the 'silver surfers' would have to be checked with the Criminal Records Bureau (CRB) before the young volunteers could be recruited. Reluctantly, this was felt to be too much of a hassle, and in any case unacceptable and inappropriate, so the idea was scrapped.[82]

The growth and reach of child protection initiatives are among the more striking changes in the UK's public policy landscape. In the past, those tackling child abuse focused on family interventions, but recent years have seen the introduction of broader measures and a very different approach. The most prominent of these are the Sex Offenders' Register, set up in 1997, and the Criminal Records Bureau, launched in 2002. These developments are cited as evidence that society is taking child abuse more seriously and, until recently, they would have met with almost unanimous support. However, as the net has widened, cogent concerns about the scope of child protection are beginning to be raised.

The Safeguarding Vulnerable Groups Act 2006 creates a whole new bureaucracy to regulate contact between children and other vulnerable groups on the one hand, and adult workers and volunteers on the other. The Act, which puts into place the legislative measures prompted by the Bichard inquiry into the 2002 Soham murders, defines a broad range of 'regulated activities' that require anyone carrying them out to be vetted. Regulated activities are those that are 'carried out frequently [i.e. once a week or more], on three or more days in a 30-day period, or overnight', and either involve contact with children or take place on specified premises. The Government estimates that the new regulatory regime will for the first time extend mandatory vetting to over two million volunteers and workers involved in sports and leisure activities, and over 200,000 school governors. In effect, the Act places around nine million adults technically under suspicion of abuse: a third of the adult working population. Once this legislation comes into effect the annual running costs of the system – already £83 million in 2005/6 – are expected to rise.[83] The costs will largely be paid by volunteer groups and schools, providing a further deterrent to the use of volunteers to work with children.

The Government has not given any estimates of how many cases of child abuse will be prevented, though it admits that 'the new scheme on its own will not completely prevent all such abuse in the workplace.'[84] It is likely to be a tiny number compared to the abuse that still takes place in domestic settings. In 2000, the National Society for the Prevention of Cruelty to Children (NSPCC) surveyed a representative sample of over 2,000 18 to 24-year-olds, using a methodology designed to record maltreatment across all parts of their lives. Sexual abuse by people who fit the categories of abuser newly covered by the Act hardly registered.[85] In comparison, the NSPCC estimates that around 79 children a year – between one and two a week – are being killed by their parents or others in their families: a rate that, despite decades of effort, is as high as ever.[86]

The child protection system places great weight on the need to follow procedures. The CRB check is widely seen as the 'gold standard' that induces public confidence in the cleared person: so much so that some parents have even started to use it to vet shop staff that their children might come into contact with.[87] However, a clear CRB check is no guarantee that a person is not a threat. Much, perhaps most, child abuse goes unreported and undetected. Hence CRB checks will miss many people who might abuse. Unless detection and conviction rates improve massively, CRB checks will continue to give far less protection than many people think, even if every adult in the country is vetted.

This reliance on a technical, bureaucratic procedure may ultimately leave children less well protected. For organisations, failure to carry out appropriate checks means facing a fine of up to £5,000. Many agencies will therefore focus solely on carrying out checks at the expense of other measures, such as training and awareness-raising, which could be more effective in protecting children from abuse. When compliance becomes simply a matter of following procedures, there is little or no room for the application of judgement and common sense. In his 2004 book, *The Risk Management of Everything*, Professor Michael Power, Director of the Centre for Analysis of Risk and Regulation at the London School of Economics, set out the dangers of secondary risk management, where organisations become more concerned to show they have followed the correct procedures than to take effective action. He argued that secondary risk management can lead to 'a potentially catastrophic downward spiral in which expert judgement shrinks to an empty form of defendable compliance.'[88]

Meanwhile, the wider implications of the expanded regime could be significant. In such a large bureaucracy mistakes are inevitable, and when millions of people are in the system the numbers affected can be high. Home Office figures from 2006 showed that the CRB wrongly labelled 2,700 people as criminals: many consequently had job offers withdrawn.[89] The existing procedures are already having an impact on recruitment in the volunteering sector.[90] Some potential employees or volunteers with irrelevant convictions are likely to worry about their details becoming public, so they may either fail to put themselves forward or pull out when the question of CRB checks is raised. Others may resent being asked, with the same result.

The prospect of unintended consequences has begun to worry some of those who have always been at the forefront of initiatives to tackle child abuse. Celia Brackenridge, former Olympic sportswoman and one of the architects of child protection policies in sport, said in 2006:

> 'Having been one of the major advocates for a long, long time, we have got to
> the point where I am saying "whoah, slow down a bit" because it has got out of
> hand in some areas. People say, "We are not going to run our junior club" or
> "Nobody will drive the bus."'[91]

This resentment with the extensive vetting process points to a possible longer-term side-effect. The attempt to regulate contact between adults and children will, if taken too far, undermine the very bonds of mutual trust that make communities welcoming, safe places for children. The next section, on fear of strangers, develops this argument.

The motivation behind the expansion of child protection is understandable. It is, at least in part, the expression of a natural outrage at the repellent behaviour of repeat abusers. Not only are they determined to gain access to children whom they can then abuse, but they persist even after their actions have become known. However, this outrage can lead to the view that the pursuit of abusers is justified whatever the cost or consequences. The danger is that policymakers may focus excessively on attempts to insulate children from all adults who might possibly harm them, and to neglect other ways of helping children to keep themselves safe from abuse, or to cope when abuse happens.

Fear of strangers

The depth of the fear of strangers shows beyond reasonable doubt that human beings do not take an actuarial position on risk. As the leading risk theorist Professor John Adams has pointed out, while society as a whole appears to be relatively sanguine about car crashes, we are highly intolerant of murder, even though we are much more likely to be killed in a car crash than murdered.[92] The murder of a child by someone they do not know is among the rarest of crimes, but its emotional power is such that even to prompt discussion about levels of risk can appear insensitive. Yet such discussion is important in gaining perspective.

Around five to seven children a year are killed by strangers.[93] Looking at children in the 5 to 11 age range (who, as we saw in Chapter 1, have experienced a dramatic loss of freedom, partly as a result of the fear of strangers), unpublished government figures show that, on average, two primary schoolchildren are killed by strangers each year.

The Home Office data on which this second statistic is based gives the numbers and ages of murder victims, aged under 16 years, killed by strangers in England and Wales for each year between 1995 and 2004/5.[94] It shows that in 1995 not a single child between 5 and 11 was killed by a stranger. By contrast, in 2002/3 four children of primary school age were killed by a stranger. But there is no trend: in each of the two years following 2002/3 there was just one case. The annual figure changes randomly throughout the 11-year period.

In fact, the figures have been at around their current level for decades.[95] Precisely because the crime is so rare, it can be stated with near certainty that there are no more predatory child killers at large today than there were in 1990 or 1975. These statistics categorically refute the dominant media message that dangerous, predatory strangers represent a significant or growing threat to children.

Yet the public believes the threat is dangerous and growing. This assessment, suggested by the most cursory glance at the tabloid press, is reinforced by the findings of public surveys. Frank Furedi, Professor of Sociology at the University of Kent, and a prominent commentator on contemporary public anxieties, quotes research commissioned by the BBC in Scotland in the late 1990s:

> 'Although the incidence of child murder by a stranger in Scotland is very low and had shown no change in the past 20 years, 76 per cent of respondents thought

SAY **NO** TO STRANGERS

that there had been an increase in such tragedies, while 38 per cent believed that the increase had been "dramatic".[96]

As already noted, far more children – between one and two a week – are killed by their parents or by other adults who know them. A 2003 Home Office report found that for every child under 16 years killed by a stranger, 14 were killed by people they knew.[97] As with playground fatalities, or indeed any child deaths, such statistics are no consolation to those whose lives are destroyed by loss. Yet here, too, public policy needs to be guided by more than the impulse to sympathise and a simplistic wish to make things better. In their book *Innocence Betrayed: Paedophilia, the media and society*, the journalist Jon Silverman and criminologist David Wilson argue that there is an urgent need to correct what they call a 'corrosive imbalance in society's thinking'. This means:

> 'acknowledging that our children are, statistically, at no greater risk in the year
> 2002 than they were in 1972 of being abducted and killed by a stranger, but that
> they remain unacceptably vulnerable to sexual abuse and exploitation by people
> whom they should be able to trust without question.'[98]

Children also suffer lesser, though still damaging, abuse, victimisation and harassment from strangers. In the late 1990s, a team of researchers led by Bernard Gallagher at the University of Huddersfield asked a sample of children aged 9 to 16 years from north-west England about their experiences of sexual abuse outside the home – the first study of its kind.[99] They found that 9 per cent had experienced what they called a 'stranger-perpetrated sexual incident' at some time in their lives. A slightly higher proportion had been the victim of similar incidents perpetrated by someone they knew, usually other children and young people.

The researchers found that indecent exposure was by far the most common type of incident. Around 2 per cent of the sample said that someone had 'tried to make them go with them', and a similar proportion had been touched in a sexual way. Of the sample of 2,420 children, four said that they had been abducted, while a single child mentioned

---

OPPOSITE: Signs such as this one at a public playground may be well-intentioned, but their uncompromising message fuels fear and mistrust. Photo: Tim Gill.

having been made to touch a stranger in a sexual way. The researchers concluded that the findings 'offer some reassurance, with only a small minority of children experiencing such incidents and many of the reported incidents involving "less serious" acts.'

The research also showed that children are capable of protecting themselves from sexual victimisation. It found that 'ten times as many perpetrators tried to get children to go with them as achieved this' with a similar ratio in relation to sexual touching. Another report using the same sample showed that the bulk of unwelcome or hostile behaviour that children face stems from other children. A small proportion involves any level of sexual threat from strangers, and the great majority of these are failed attempts.[100]

Sexual attacks and harassment by strangers are at the very least unpleasant experiences for children: in the study quoted above, almost three-quarters of victims said they had been very or quite frightened. For those few children actually abducted, the experience – and the anguish felt by family and friends – is extremely traumatic. Clinical studies show that for child sexual abuse in general, aside from any physical trauma, the psychological consequences can be profound, including post-traumatic stress disorder and long-term behavioural, emotional and sex and relationship problems. Yet other things being equal, the prospects for recovery are usually better with stranger abuse than when the perpetrator is known to the child. When a child knows their abuser, the psychological impact can be worse because so often it involves the destruction of the child's sense of trust.[101]

Statistically, the pattern of abuse, harassment and distress inflicted on children by strangers shows the same pyramid shape as for other types of risk. At its apex is a vanishingly small number of deaths at the hands of violent, predatory paedophiles. The next tier down includes a larger but still proportionately small number of abductions and serious sexual assaults. At the base of the triangle is a still larger group of episodes of less serious sexual maltreatment and harassment. The most common manifestation of the threat to children from strangers today accords with many people's childhood memories of 'the neighbourhood flasher'. Many, perhaps most, communities have within them some people who are prone to be sexually threatening to children they have no real connection with. The bulk of crimes they commit, while distressing, are of a type that children can recover from well. It is also clear from the findings of the Gallagher study quoted above that only a minority of such people progress to more serious crimes.

It is true that the tiny number of violent, predatory paedophiles that are at large do not come with easy-to-read ID tags that enable people to tell them apart from those who represent a lesser threat. However, to jump from that truth to the claim that anyone who flashes at a child might turn out to be a child murderer is simply scaremongering. There are legitimate questions about how to manage the risk from sex offenders. However, they will not be explored further here, for reasons of space and because there has already been much public policy discussion on this topic.

The fact is that fear of strangers itself has unhealthy consequences for children. At its most prosaic level it leaves many parents and children unnecessarily anxious. It reinforces a norm of parenting that equates being a good parent with being a controlling parent, and that sees the granting of independence as a sign of indifference if not outright neglect, even though the benefits of giving children a degree of freedom to play, especially outside, are increasingly well documented.[102] Where families are under emotional stress through poverty, poor housing or domestic problems, parents and children both benefit if the children can spend time outside the home. The retreat from the outdoors denies children the chance to build their confidence and competences through everyday interactions with the wider world, which some argue could adversely affect their mental health.[103]

Excessive fear of strangers, like excessive fear of sexual abuse, can corrode the very ties that help communities to be safe and convivial for both adults and children. The question of how strangers of all ages treat each other was a central concern for Jane Jacobs, one of the twentieth-century's leading thinkers on city planning and urban life. In her classic 1961 book *The Death and Life of Great American Cities* she states that 'the first fundamental of successful city life' is that 'people must take a modicum of public responsibility for each other even if they have no ties to each other.' And she goes on:

> 'This is a lesson nobody learns by being told. It is learned from the experience of having other people without ties of kinship or close friendship or formal respon- sibility to you take a modicum of responsibility for you.'[104]

The vast majority of adults do not intend to harm children they do not know, so strangers are a largely dependable source of help if things go wrong. Safety messages that warn children never to speak to strangers reinforce the view that it is wrong for adults to initiate social contact with children they don't know. A tragic event from 2002 shows where such attitudes can lead. A two-year-old girl named Abigail Rae escaped unnoticed from her nursery. Soon afterwards she was found drowned in a nearby pond after falling in. During the inquest it emerged that a man passing by had seen her wandering the streets on her own, but had done nothing. He told the inquest: 'One of the reasons I did not go back is because I thought someone would see me and think I was trying to abduct her.'[105]

Some child safety materials continue to highlight the threat from strangers, and to reinforce the message that strangers are not to be trusted. For instance, a leaflet for parents entitled *Keep Them Safe*, available from the website of the child safety charity Kidscape, makes no clear reference to the subject of domestic abuse, apart from the risk from baby-sitters and the admonishment to children that they should tell if someone tries to harm them, even if it is someone they know. It should be noted that other Kidscape initiatives specifically address domestic abuse and this leaflet is designed to give general messages about personal safety. However, its message about strangers is unequivocal: 'It is NEVER a good idea to talk to a stranger.''[106]

Initiatives have emerged that are relevant to a wide range of abusive situations and that do not give misleading messages about the relative risks. One such approach, known as Protective Behaviours, has been taken up by the child welfare charity Barnardo's. This approach first emerged in the USA in the 1970s, before spreading via Australia to the UK in the 1990s, and aims to help children to develop their ability to take effective action when they feel they are not safe. A key impetus behind Protective Behaviours was the fact noted above that, while the vast majority of child abuse takes place in the family, education programmes for children focus overwhelmingly on the threat from strangers. Protective Behaviours explicitly aims to 'reframe our language into an empowering, non-victimising and non-violent format'. The UK website for the practitioner network describes it as 'a practical and down-to-earth approach to child safety' that 'encourages self-empowerment and brings with it the skills to avoid being victimised'. The statement continues:

> 'This is achieved by helping people recognise and trust their intuitive feelings (early warning signs) and develop strategies for self-protection. The Protective Behaviours process encourages an adventurous approach to life which satisfies the need for fun and excitement without violence and fear.'

Protective Behaviours emphasises the difference between feeling safe, adventurousness, risking on purpose and feeling unsafe. It argues that these differences are manifested by what it calls early warning signs: specific bodily responses that signal when we do not feel safe. The approach also encourages everyone to develop their personal networks of support, and to explore letting people know we need to talk to them.[107]

Online risks

Technological advances are transforming the lives of children at a bewildering rate, in itself a source of anxiety for adults who, unlike children, tend to struggle to master the new technologies of the internet and mobile phones. The assumed order of things – by which adults hold the keys to knowledge and experience – is largely inverted when it comes to the digital world.

Sonia Livingstone, Professor of Social Psychology at the London School of Economics, is an authority on children's relationship with new technology. In her view the internet 'has rapidly become central in children's lives, and ... represents a significant addition to the existing means of communication open to them.'[108] While this is true, the process is still underway, and has not yet spread as far as some commentators imply. The internet is out of everyday reach to large sections of the child population: in 2006 39 per cent of households had no internet access at all, while only around 45 per cent had the high-speed broadband connections that much of the worldwide web now depends upon.[109] It is only in the last few years that even a minority of children have made online activities a feature of their daily lives.

However, a 2007 report from the think tank Demos confirmed that the internet is becoming central to children's social lives, in the form of instant messaging and social networking sites like BeBo. It is also a key location for information gathering and informal learning, through search engines and online reference sites; a forum for generating and sharing creative content, through blogs and sites like MySpace and YouTube; and a growing focus for other leisure activities such as online multiplayer games and special-interest sites.[110]

The Demos report also showed that for some children and young people, the internet is not just a medium for entertainment and social networking, it is new territory for creativity, exploration and adventure. It highlights the emergence of a group of young people it labelled 'digital pioneers' who are at the forefront of developing new ways of creating, sharing and using content.

As the Demos report argues, children's mastery of online technology will be crucial not just for their social and leisure lives and education, but also for their future economic prospects. Even if it were possible to isolate children from the online world, to do so would unquestionably have damaging consequences for them and for society as a whole.

The digital world holds threats as well as promises. The threats come in three forms: online child sexual abuse; violent and/or sexual images, video and other content that in itself upsets or damages children; and so-called cyberbullying. All these are harmful, yet the vast majority of children enjoy rich, active online lives without suffering any serious or long-term harm from them.

Of the three, it is online sex offending that gives rise to the greatest adult anxieties. It is the central concern of the Child Exploitation and Online Protection Centre (CEOP), set up by the Government in 2006. While the media sometimes give the impression that predatory sex offenders are a significant danger, CEOP admits that the level of threat is in reality 'incredibly difficult to define'.[111] It notes that 'the biggest risk to children and young people is self-generated, frequently caused by providing too much personal information or by behaviour which presents an opportunity for victimisation.' There is a clear tension here between the advice given by many child safety agencies not to share personal information, or not to meet with new online contacts, and the reality of how children are using the internet as part of their social lives. Take the question of children arranging meetings with people they initially encountered online. Government-funded research shows that 25 per cent of children and young people had done this.[112] It also found that around three-quarters of those took someone else with them, indicating that they were aware of the risks. However, 85 per cent chose to take a friend rather than a trusted adult, parent or family member, which, CEOP argued, showed that children are taking unnecessary risks. CEOP concluded that 'there is a need to provide further advice to children and young people on who is best placed to protect them in a potentially abusive situation.' Yet it could equally be argued that choosing to take a friend was the most sensible action as it is unrealistic to suggest that parents should always accompany children on significant social activities. The advice may even undermine children's safety, since parents who try to put this rule into practice may push their children into making secret arrangements rather than at least keeping them informed.

With regard to the threat from online content – especially violent content – the debate takes a form that is familiar to those with a historical perspective on the relationship between children and mass media. The internet is largely unregulated – though this is changing – and the indisputable repulsiveness of some material accessible on line is, for many, evidence enough that children should be prevented from viewing it. However, as Hugh Cunningham notes in *The Invention of Childhood*, the emergence of each new popular medium, from 'penny dreadfuls' through cinema and television to videos, computer games and now a new set of online activities, has been paralleled by heated, morally charged and often unrevealing debate about their influence on that generation of children.[113]

In September 2007, in the wake of growing public concern about gang violence involving young people, Prime Minister Gordon Brown announced a consultation on the effects of the media on children.[114] As other such initiatives have shown, this is highly contested territory. In 2006, Sonia Livingstone and media regulation expert Andrea Millwood Hargrave published a review of the effects of media content.[115] This was wide-ranging, covering evidence from academic, industry and regulatory sources across all types of new media and for audiences of all ages.

The review emphasises the crucial but often-neglected distinction between harm, which is objective, long-term and observable by others (in principle at least), and offence, which is subjective, more immediate and more difficult to measure reliably. The authors argue that, notwithstanding this problem of measurement, drawing conclusions about offence is fairly straightforward, but drawing conclusions about harm is not. They noted the real methodological difficulties – in showing cause and effect, in applying laboratory findings to the real world, and applying results from one audience group or medium to others – and the 'patchy and inconsistent' nature of the evidence base.[116]

Millwood Hargrave and Livingstone tentatively conclude that the research literature points to a range of modest effects, including 'effects on attitudes and beliefs, effects on emotions, and, more controversially, effects on behaviour (or the predisposition towards certain behaviours).'[117] They support the common-sense position that children warrant a special focus, stating that 'research findings do suggest that vulnerable audiences/users may include children and young people, especially boys.'[118]

They note that the widespread accessibility, affordability, anonymity and convenience of the internet marks an important difference from other media and that

In 2007 Prime Minister Gordon Brown announced a review of the effects of the internet and computer games on children, to be led by clinical psychologist and TV presenter Dr Tanya Byron. The apparent ease with which children can master the technology, and the access it can provide to violent, disturbing or pornographic material, make this an especially challenging arena for adults. Photo: www.johnbirdsall.co.uk.

this explains the heightened concerns over more extreme forms of content. However, their strongest conclusion is that debates need to move beyond simplistic arguments about cause and effect. Instead they call for a more sophisticated analysis: one that brings together the broad range of factors – including content, audience, medium, viewing situation and social context – that might combine to produce unwanted behaviour and undesirable outcomes.[119]

Apart from any direct influences from the content of new media, children who are heavy consumers can also be affected in other, negative, ways – for example, the experiences they miss out on because of the time they spend gaming, listening or watching. However, some arguments about the 'opportunity costs' of such online activities make wrong assumptions about how children pursue them. For instance, game-playing is often highly social, with tactics and strategy being the subject of much lively debate amongst friends and peers. Overall, the consequences of spending a lot of time online may for many – though not all – children be no more or less concerning than the impact of pursuing many other sedentary, indoor activities to excess.

Cyberbullying – through texting, sharing photos or videos, email and social networking website – is in essence an old form of victimisation in a new context. Millward Hargrave and Livingstone argue that it is too soon to know whether this new technology has led to an overall increase in such practices.[120] There are some obvious differences: perpetrators can remain anonymous, and online bullying can be a more public form of humiliation and potentially create a permanent record. A less obvious difference is that children taking part in online social engagements of all kinds are, like everyone else, operating in a context in which some of the rules and conventions are unclear, even unresolved. This makes the questions raised earlier in this chapter, about where to draw the line between acceptable and unacceptable behaviour, even more difficult – though the line does need to be drawn.

A common message to parents from agencies in this field is that they should take active steps to monitor their children. A range of software products and internet services are available that claim to help keep children safe online. However, some experts question the value of this advice and the technical fixes on offer. The Demos authors point out that filters are 'vulnerable to advances in technology and digitally savvy children' and that moreover 'the children we interviewed were aware of potential dangers and adept at self-regulating.' Livingstone argues that:

'Simply pressing for more parental monitoring, restriction and control could encourage children's evasion rather than their cooperation with attempts at internet regulation in the home.'[121]

The virtual world demands the same thoughtful approach to balancing risks and benefits as any of the real-world contexts already discussed. As Sonia Livingstone argues, 'online opportunities and risks for children must be considered together.'[122] Risk elimination is no more possible here than anywhere else in childhood. It is especially futile to base responses on the premise that children are in some global sense vulnerable. In their online lives, children are successfully learning and sharing ways to pursue their interests, while keeping themselves safe.

Conclusions

The topics explored in this chapter provide further illustrations of some of the themes already noted in connection with playground safety. Policy and practice are often focused on the goal of reducing adverse outcomes, when there is a manifest need to take into account the benefits of allowing children more freedom to explore, discover, take a degree of responsibility and experience risks for themselves. Rare, tragic adverse outcomes have a disproportionate influence, with scant regard to evidence and little or no debate about how to draw the line between these and more common, less serious experiences. Safety initiatives tend to take the form of quick fixes, technical or bureau-cratic procedures that work against the exercise of judgement. Moreover, little or no consideration is given to the possible side-effects of measures that will lead to further restrictions and limitations on children's lives. Underpinning and connecting all these topics is an assumption of children's vulnerability (or in the case of antisocial behaviour, their villainy) combined with a lack of interest in how to foster their resilience and sense of responsibility. The next chapter explores why these adult attitudes have emerged.

CHAPTER 4

Who is to blame?

Chapters 2 and 3 concluded that our growing aversion to childhood risks is essentially the result of a collective failure of nerve about children's need to learn for themselves how to cope with many types of risk. Chapter 4 argues that for parents this failure of nerve is an understandable side-effect of wider social and cultural changes. However, for other adults – teachers, childcare workers, activity leaders – it is compounded by the fear of being blamed and by the over-regulation and institutionalisation of childhood. This chapter also explores the changing role of the media in influencing perceptions and shaping debates.

Parents

According to a 2006 report from the Future Foundation, the time parents spend looking after their children each day has quadrupled from 25 minutes in 1975 to 99 minutes in 2000. This is more than an hour extra every day. It also showed that the public believe the opposite: that parents spend less time with their children than they used to. The report suggests that the increase in time spent on childcare is in part because of growing parental anxiety, and that 'previous generations were less worried about letting children play alone in the garden or in the streets.'[123] This might suggest that parents must take some responsibility for the increasing overprotectiveness of children. However, there are good arguments for thinking that, while parents as a group may be conduits of risk aversion, they are not the source. Most parents are well aware that part of their job is to help their children prepare for life as an autonomous adult, and that this process involves a gradual transfer of power. Whatever their initial views about their children's vulnerability, sooner or later parents have to respond to their offsprings' demands for greater everyday responsibility.

A host of social and cultural changes have made this transfer of power from parent to child more difficult. Perhaps foremost amongst these is traffic danger, which has left most residential streets more dangerous and unpleasant. It is a legitimate fear for parents. Although child pedestrian casualties have been falling for many years, there is clear evidence that this is simply because there are fewer children out and about in the streets. As a 2001 UNICEF report on child deaths by injury notes:

> 'Telling parents that they are being overprotective and that the roads are becoming safer for their children is, in this context, like telling them that they can let their children play with matches again because deaths from fire have been falling.'[124]

Meanwhile fear of crime and strangers, and other less specific fears, have made all public spaces feel less safe. These factors, combined with our appetite for digital and consumer cultures, mean that family life is now lived increasingly under cover: inside the home, and in cars, shops and indoor leisure facilities. As a result, residential streets and public spaces can be largely devoid of people, especially parents and children. In addition, greater mobility has resulted in more transient populations in many areas.[125]

For many children and parents, therefore, the immediate neighbourhood around the family home is no longer populated with familiar faces. They may have never met, said hello to, or perhaps even set eyes on their neighbours. As parents today look out of their front doors, they see a world that is at best uninterested in their children and at worst hostile to them. Fewer friendly faces mean that support and solidarity from other adults, even in the minimal form of a watching eye, can rarely be assumed.

These societal changes have radically altered the norms of good parenting for parents of children up to their teenage years. Children are expected to be under the active care of a responsible adult, either a parent or someone implicitly or explicitly 'contracted' to assume the role. The idea of benign neglect – by which parents elect to give their children time and space beyond the purview of any assigned adults – has all but disappeared from acceptable parenting practice. Frank Furedi, sociologist and author of *Paranoid Parenting*, argues that:

> 'Parents are almost forced to fall in line… The minority of parents who try to resist it are stigmatised as irresponsible. When your own kid is the only one allowed to go shopping, to go to the swimming pool by himself, it looks very strange.'[126]

In loco parentis

As the legal term *in loco parentis* makes clear, the parent-child relationship provides a yardstick for many other relationships between children and significant adults in their lives. The courts apply the benchmark of a 'reasonable parent' in making judgements, for instance, about the responsibility of a teacher in a classroom or on a school trip. As parents adopt a parenting culture in which someone is expected to be in charge, so a high degree of supervision and control has become the norm for other adults in positions of responsibility for children, such as teachers, childcare workers or outdoor activity leaders. Different parents will have different norms and expectations, but workers and agencies may feel under pressure to accede to the demands of the most risk averse unless their professional values and objectives give them the confidence to resist this.

Girlguiding UK has vast experience of the dynamic and evolving relationship between parents and volunteer adult leaders who take on responsibility for their children. Jennie Lamb, former Head of Guiding Development at the Association, has worked in guiding for 20 years. In her view, one of the biggest issues for the movement is the need for young women to learn how to take risks themselves, and know when to stop. In an interview for this book she gave one example of the parental pressure that Guide leaders encounter in trying to address this question:

> 'Sometimes when we run residentials, we let the girls bring some money and we often take them on a visit to a shopping centre. The tradition ... has always been that Brownies [from around seven years of age] would always be with a leader, but Guides would be given some freedom, and our break is between 10 and 11. But now you will have the 11 or 12-year-old's parent saying "You're not going to let my daughter go shopping without you in Brentwood High Street." And we say, "Yes we are, we'll sit in the middle on the seats outside the shops, and they'll go off in threes and fours, and they'll have an hour, and they'll come back – but if they need us we'll be sitting there the whole time." Some parents feel the Guides are prepared to give [their children] more freedom than they are and they are not sure that that's right.'

Schools

In schools, the effects of risk aversion can be seen inside and outside the classroom. With regard to the curriculum, concerns have been voiced about the impact on learning of risk averse attitudes and regulations in subjects as diverse as science, art and sports.[127] But of greater interest to the current discussion is the growing debate about risk aversion beyond the classroom: on school trips and related activities, and in the playground.

Education outside the classroom was the subject of a 2005 House of Commons Education and Skills Select Committee report that examined a wide range of outdoor learning experiences, from lessons held in school grounds to expeditions abroad.[128] The report found that 'in England in 2003, there were between seven and ten million "pupil visits" involving educational or recreational activity, but only one fatality.' It noted that these statistics 'compare extremely favourably with other routine activities such as driving or being driven in a car, or simply the likelihood of an accident at home or in school'. In spite of these statistics, and the widespread support for outdoor learning, the Select Committee stated that there has been a general decline in both the quantity and quality of opportunities for outdoor education, which 'seems to be affecting all types of outdoor experience'. It argued that the lack of such experiences 'impoverishes students' learning and represents a missed opportunity for curricular enrichment'.

The Select Committee concluded that 'the sector is burdened by excessive bureaucracy, a low profile and a distorted perception of risk that is not supported by the facts.' It stated that 'some schools and local authorities are demanding excessively lengthy risk assessments and we have found evidence of needless duplication in the system.' The picture that emerges is of widespread overreaction to a small number of incidents where there may have been safety failings. A regime of secondary risk management has developed in which the different agencies involved – school, local education authority, destination, Ofsted and government departments – appear to be more concerned to defend themselves against accusations of poor practice than to work together to support learning activities while managing the risks in an effective way.

The Education Select Committee identified some successful attempts to transcend risk aversion. It was particularly impressed by the 'forest school' initiative, which involves offering groups of children regular opportunities for hands-on learning in a woodland setting as part of their school curriculum.[129] The Committee noted how this approach 'uses the environment as a tool to enrich the curriculum, whilst enabling students to experience a carefully monitored element of risk and to become more familiar with the natural world'. Forest schools originated in Sweden in the 1950s. They spread across Scandinavia, especially in Denmark where the model became a mainstream response to the expansion of pre-school education, partly due to a shortage of suitable buildings.[130]

Forest schools first appeared in the UK in the mid 1990s. Exact figures are not available, but the total number of projects in the UK probably numbers in the hundreds.[131] While they are still less widespread than in Denmark or Sweden, their growing number is a sign that risk aversion can be challenged. Two factors help explain the model's success. First, it has a clear ethos, which includes an appreciation of the value of woodland settings as challenging, stimulating environments, and a holistic approach to learning in which children enjoy relative freedom to explore the setting and develop their confidence and competences in ways that are meaningful to them.[132] Second, forest school leaders receive specialist training in forest school values and approaches and how to apply them.

Like school trips, school play and break times have been in decline for some years. Psychologists Antony Pellegrini and Peter Blatchford found that between 1990 and 1995/6, the lunchtime break had been reduced by an average of 38 per cent in English junior schools and by 26 per cent in primary schools. Afternoon breaks had been eliminated in 27 per cent of junior, 12 per cent of infant and 14 per cent of primary schools.[133] Some secondary schools have eliminated unstructured breaks altogether, or propose to. Amongst these is the Thomas Deacon Academy in Peterborough, the most expensive state-funded school ever built in England and one of the Government's flagship academies, whose plans for breaks were the subject of widespread media discussion, some of it critical, when they emerged in May 2007.[134] For many children these periods are their only regular opportunities to spend time with friends and peers, and so are valuable parts of their school lives. Summarising research on the issue, Pellegrini has stated:

> 'When kids go to school, they find something that they are good at... In fact, what recess is allowing these kids to do is to exhibit confidence in a relatively foreign, in many ways literally foreign environment. They are exhibiting confidence.'[135]

Reductions in school trips, breaks and playtimes are caused in part by anxieties about children and risk, expressed by many professionals as a fear of being blamed. Teachers and schools are also vulnerable to the expectation from some parents that education should be entirely free of risk. For instance, one teachers union, the NASUWT, advises its members to consider carefully whether or not to participate in non-contractual educational visits and journeys 'because of the great personal and professional risks involved'.[136] However, another cause is that schools are now under increasing pressure to show that they are measurably improving children's learning, principally through their performance in standardised tests and public examinations. 'I think what the public want is maximum learning,' stated the head of the Thomas Deacon Academy in defending the school's decision not to have a playground.

A school playground in Berlin which gives children the chance to challenge their abilities. Photo: Nils Norman.

The charity Playlink argued in an action research report in 1999 that when schools think of playtime as a break from learning rather than as a positive, valued contribution to the day, 'play will be marginalised and seen through the distorting prism of "behaviour management" and the need for games-based activities.'[137] Even in the early years, where outdoor play has traditionally been more highly valued, the focus on results has in the opinion of child psychologist Jennie Lindon 'pushed outdoor play and related physical play to the sidelines'.[138] Creative Partnerships, the Government's programme to raise the educational profile of creative practice, shows that there may not be any great tension between time spent outside the classroom, where many of their activities take place (whether for learning or play), and educational performance.[139] However, it is hard for many schools and teachers to resist the logic of the argument that more classroom time will improve results.

Settings beyond the school

Voluntary and community activities have remained a relatively constant feature of children's out-of-school lives in recent years, but organisations providing structured outdoor activities for children are at the sharp end of debates about risk aversion. The Scout and Guide Associations in particular – by far the largest providers – have been active on the issue, submitting evidence to Parliamentary inquiries and supporting campaigns for legislative reform. They have also made strenuous efforts to take – and defend – a robust approach to risk with parents and volunteers, and with some success, as the quote from Jennie Lamb showed (see page 64). For instance, in 2006 Girlguiding UK issued risk management guidance to local leaders – the backbone of the organisation – that argued for a balanced approach. This document was influenced by the Play Safety Forum's statement *Managing Risk in Play Provision* (see page 35), particularly its emphasis on the need to take into account the benefits of activities as well as the risks.[140]

For both pre-school and school-age children, the last decade has seen a dramatic expansion in the time spent in formal childcare. The main reasons for this expansion have been economic, not educational. As a result, the regulatory framework and guidance have had a strong focus on minimum standards for safety and security, with arguably less emphasis on the nature of the experience. For instance, there are no statutory requirements for childcare settings to include outdoor space.

If childcare workers believe that their overriding priority is to return children to their parents unscathed, there will inevitably be little incentive to allow children to experiment, explore or step beyond their comfort zones. For workers, permitting a child to do things that might lead to hurt or distress means taking a risk themselves, so they are likely to supervise children closely and direct and control their activities.

This tendency to overprotection is reinforced by the low status of childcare as a profession. Entry qualifications are far less demanding than for teaching, youth work or social work, and, once employed, most childcare workers have little or no non-contact time for reflection and planning. Staff often do not have the grounding in child development that might help them to assess risk in a balanced way, nor do they have the opportunity to discuss and improve their practice. There is also a high staff turnover in many childcare settings. As a result, staff will struggle to develop the kind of long-term relationships with children that would help them to make sound judgements about the risks that these children might be capable of handling. The situation would be improved if staff had higher status, more demanding entry qualifications and better pay and conditions – proposals that are being debated.

The pressure on out-of-school settings to reduce risk can be resisted. The staffed adventure playground is one form of out-of-school provision that has explicitly embraced challenging, self-directed experiences and comparatively risky forms of outdoor play. Adventure playgrounds – inspired by observations of children playing on bombsites – emerged in wartime Denmark, first came to the UK in the 1960s and then spread in the 1970s and 80s, especially in disadvantaged neighbourhoods. They originally consisted largely of a constantly changing array of self-built structures made from whatever materials were to hand, the processes of creation and destruction being as important as the results. Since the 1980s many adventure playgrounds have closed, though there are still perhaps a hundred or more in existence in the UK. Many of those that remain are valued local facilities, and the best offer rich environments for play and informal learning. However, the free-form 'junk playground' has all but disappeared, in part due to a climate of risk aversion. Nevertheless, the expanding profession of 'playwork' has emerged from the understanding and expertise of adventure playworkers, and is influential in a range of out-of-school childcare settings. The charity

Play Wales, for instance, has drawn up a set of UK-wide 'principles of playwork' that make explicit the playworker's role in fostering children's confidence and allowing them to explore boundaries and take risks.[141]

In Scandinavia, childcare looks quite different. The offer to children is much wider than in the UK with more emphasis on children taking control and responsibility.[142] The workers – known as 'pedagogues', a name that identifies their role as facilitators of children's learning and development – are more highly qualified and have better pay and conditions than their UK counterparts, and their profession is recognised. The difference in ethos is even clear in the name of the service. Across Scandinavia, out-of-school childcare centres are known as 'free-time clubs', an acknowledgement that they are more than simply an adjunct to the school day.

Scandinavian countries have a long tradition of emphasising the importance of outdoor environments in which children are given the freedom to learn through exploration and discovery. Forest schools have already been mentioned, as have Danish adventure playgrounds. Unlike their British counterparts, these *byggelege-pladsens* – literally 'construction playgrounds' – have generally maintained the ethos of the junk playground with its landscape of self-built structures, and aim to give children practical, hands-on experience of building and of engaging with nature and the elements.

While forest schools and adventure playgrounds are more common in Denmark than in the UK, they are not universal. However, their ethos and influence is visible in other settings. On a visit to Idrætsfritidsklubben, a large free-time club outside Copenhagen, I asked project leader Henrik Perregaard how he saw his role. He explained that in simple terms, it was 'to give children a place where they can be after school in a more free way, to be with their friends and to build up good friendships. A place where they can enjoy things and life.' But he added:

> 'If I look deeper, it is my job to get children out from here with a feeling of
> taking responsibility for other people and themselves. To give them skills in

---

OPPOSITE: **A newly built competition-standard skatepark in Malmö, Sweden, which is unsupervised, open all hours and free of charge to users, located in the heart of Bo01, a flagship urban regeneration area. Photo: Nils Norman.**

how to be with other people and their friends... not to be nervous when [they] meet other people.'

It would be wrong to assume that Danish pedagogues are indifferent to the urge to keep children safe, or that all take the same approach to risk and freedom. Perregaard was clear that the question was one of balance:

'I think if you draw a line, on one part of the line you have your responsibility – this is my responsibility for the children, I must take care, nothing must happen to this child... The other part is how can I give this child experience, how can I give him responsibility. It depends how your focus is. Are you more on one side of the line or on the other side? Here we think more of how to give them experiences and so on. Of course we think about taking care ... but that is not our focus. I think a lot of pedagogues have too much focus on the other part.'

The media

The media have to bear some responsibility for fuelling risk aversion, as the Better Regulation Commission makes clear in *Risk, Responsibility and Regulation*. One typical example of newspaper coverage helps to highlight some of the issues. On 21 May 2006 the *Sunday Mirror* ran a story with the headline, 'Where is our Fran? Fears as girl of 10 goes missing.' It continued: 'Police were last night searching for a missing schoolgirl who has disappeared just a mile from where model Sally Anne Bowman was murdered.' In fact the missing girl, Francesca Akano, was found safe and well late that same evening, just hours after the Metropolitan Police had put out its initial statement. The Met put out a further statement to this effect, but it presumably arrived too late for the paper to pull the story. So while the child's disappearance gained prominent tabloid coverage, her reappearance was greeted with silence. Such a response is not unusual: a spokesman for the Met told me that he would not normally expect national papers to report positive outcomes under circumstances like this – especially Sunday papers, which would need to wait a week before updating readers. As far as the *Sunday Mirror*'s readership was concerned, the event was one more tragedy that reinforced the view that the world was a dangerous place for girls.

The way the media report horrific crimes involving children has changed dramatically in the last few generations. In a paper entitled 'It could happen to you', media researcher Clare Wardle compared how newspapers covered 12 similar child murder cases in the 1930s, 60s and 90s. Using material from both the UK and the US, she found that the tone of the coverage underwent a striking shift in the 1990s. Stories from this period focused heavily on the victims' families and the effect of the crimes on the wider community, resulting in coverage that was raw and emotional. The motivations for the cases were also portrayed differently: 'in the earlier periods the crimes were defined as isolated murders committed by "evil" individuals, whereas by the 1990s these crimes were considered a result of society in decline.'[143]

What this research shows is that coverage of such crimes today is more likely to heighten public fears and undermine efforts to put them in proportion than 30 or 60 years ago. Readers are more likely to be emotionally affected, and at the same time they are being told that these tragedies are not isolated incidents, but are symptomatic of a wider social problem. This powerful combination cannot help but convince many readers that they are in the midst of a rising tide of horrific abuse.

Media stories of tragedy and loss focus almost exclusively on human interest, at the expense of proportion or perspective. The senior BBC journalist Andrew Marr in his book *My Trade* bluntly gives the reasons for this preference, in a passage quoted by the Better Regulation Commission: 'To sell papers, news must move and often that means provoking fear.'[144] Nothing frightens an audience quite like seeing the world through the eyes of the victim. So parents who have experienced catastrophic loss find a willing outlet in a media with an appetite for raw emotion. Yet as the Better Regulation Commission noted in *Risk, Responsibility and Regulation*, when new public policy measures are being proposed, moving beyond emotion is vital to gaining a sense of proportion.

There are signs of a shift in attitudes to risk from at least some media quarters. Columnists and commentators of all shades of political opinion have been airing their views on the topic in growing numbers. Some newspapers have given prominent coverage to news stories of allegedly overzealous child safety initiatives. To take one pertinent example, a *Daily Mail* story from 2000 blamed playground closures on 'draconian new safety rules introduced by Brussels'.[145] In fact, as Chapter 2 discussed, the standards in question are guidelines, and were in any case less stringent than the British ones that preceded them. Nonetheless the genuine media debate prompted by such tragedies as the death in 2005 of a child killed by a falling tree in Dunham Massey Park (owned by the National Trust) points to the possibility of more balanced treatment.

Conclusions

There are significant forces pushing parents, professionals and voluntary and community agencies towards risk aversion. Where people succeed in resisting these forces it is because they have an explicit philosophy, ethos or set of values about the role of risk, experiential learning and autonomy in children's lives. The challenge for public policy is to learn from these.

In England, a policy rethink of the children's sector workforce is underway following the creation of the Children's Workforce Development Council (CWDC). This body was set up by government in 2005 as part of the 'Every Child Matters' reforms of children's services. It aims to 'ensure that the people working with children have the best possible training, qualifications, support and advice.'[146] So far the CWDC has sent out mixed messages about risk aversion. On a positive note, one of the core values it proposes (in a document on the induction of new workers) is that 'self-esteem and resilience are recognised as essential to every child's development.'[147] But there is no recognition that this necessarily involves a balanced approach to risks, and no acknowledgement that overprotective measures might themselves be harmful or unhelpful for children.

Teachers are in any case not part of the remit of the CWDC (although the restructuring of Whitehall following Gordon Brown's appointment as Prime Minister in June 2007 has brought them closer, with the creation of the new Department for Children, Schools and Families). Schools have a major role in resisting the trend to overprotect and intervene, one which is likely to increase as children spend more time within their jurisdiction. This is not just in the provision of the occasional trip or outdoor activity, but in overseeing the everyday lives of children during those periods in the school day when at least a degree of self-determination is on offer. In the context of extended schools, a balanced approach is going to be crucial in accommodating those children who are already pushing against the restrictions of the school regime.

It might appear that public policy has a harder job influencing the parental role in risk aversion, since this might be seen as a matter for parents and children to negotiate independently. Likewise, the media are not known for their willingness to engage constructively in public policy debates about their own actions and accountability. While it would take a brave government to intervene directly in these issues, there is scope for public policy to exert influence indirectly, as the concluding chapter argues.

CHAPTER 5

Beyond risk aversion

There is growing recognition that the damaging consequences of excessive risk aversion need to be tackled. The Better Regulation Commission has called for a 'more broadly based and complete dialogue, with fact and emotions more clearly distinguished'.[148] This chapter takes up the Commission's call, offering proposals for a new approach to risk in childhood. It has two overarching messages: that public policy must take seriously the need to create more child-friendly communities; and that services and institutions should reject what might be called the philosophy of protection and instead adopt a philosophy of resilience.

There is undoubtedly a small but significant number of children who are out of control, engaged in antisocial and even criminal activities and for whom repressive measures are necessary. This book, however, deals with the majority of children growing up in Britain today. Many adults both in the UK and across the developed world are aware of a stark contrast between their personal memories of childhood freedom and the constraint imposed on the lives of their own children and their peers. And they are not wrong. The picture that has emerged is that a culture of risk aversion has encroached into every aspect of children's lives – in school, in social play, in children's clubs and 'adventure' trips and in the wider public realm. Some of this is a consequence of changes in the wider world. Curiously, however, the more obvious threats to children's safety – notably that from road traffic – are not treated with anything like the same degree of obsessive control as that applied to other areas where children congregate. Car travel, it appears, is so essential and important to easing our lives that we are not prepared to apply so much rigour to the ensuing risks. The discussion on children's playgrounds in Chapter 2, in contrast, shows that where spaces can be regulated excessive controls are deemed necessary, often at great cost to the public purse and with little positive effect. It is easy to regulate a playground and even easier to lay down the law for minors who have little choice in the matter. There almost appears to be a desire to repress childhood itself.

Child Poverty in Perspective: An overview of child well-being in rich countries, a widely discussed report from UNICEF in 2007, brings together the best available data from 21 rich countries and ranks them across six dimensions of well-being.[149] The UK ranks lowest overall along with the USA; the Netherlands ranks highest, ahead of Sweden, Denmark and Finland. The UK also comes last on all the measures most relevant here: family and peer relationships; behaviours and risks; and subjective well-being.

In the UK, child health experts claim that growing numbers of children have emotional and behavioural problems by the time they reach adolescence. Research by Dr Stephan Collishaw and colleagues from the Institute of Psychiatry at King's College London, published in 2004, found evidence of increases in both conduct disorders and emotional problems amongst children and young people in the UK. Analysing large, representative databases from a number of cohort studies, they showed that the prevalence of conduct problems over the period between 1974 and 1999 had doubled, with significant increases in emotional problems over the period 1986 to 1999. The problems were widespread: by 1999 almost one in six adolescents showed what the researchers called 'more severe' conduct problems, and over one in six showed more severe emotional problems. These increases were found for both boys and girls and across all social classes and family types. By looking at longer-term outcomes the researchers argued that their findings were unlikely to be a consequence of changed reporting methods.[150]

However, such studies do beg a question about changes in public anxiety with regard to our general well-being. What were once deemed 'normal' behaviours in growing children – unruliness, tantrums, quarrels, play-fighting, shyness, introspection – seem to have become pathologised as psychological problems. While such conditions might present across a spectrum of severity from the ordinary to the medically serious, all seem to be regarded as threatening. This has consequences for children's freedom. In 1999 a Mental Health Foundation report stated that 'concern about safety and the risk of abuse or violence have limited the amount of time children play outside unsupervised, travel alone or are allowed to attend clubs and youth groups.'[151] Commenting on the report the Foundation's then director June McKerrow warned: 'there are risks to children in insulating them and not letting them develop their own coping mechanisms, or do things their own way.'[152] A sense of perspective is necessary.

Child-friendly communities

In the large, crowded conurbations many families inhabit, life feels more risky and dangerous, and parents are naturally more protective of their children. In an ideal world a radical reorganisation of the way we live might be the ultimate solution with urban planning initiatives taken to make our neighbourhoods, streets and schools more 'human scale'.[153]

OPPOSITE: **On a Bank Holiday August weekend in 1996, the residents of the Methleys in Leeds organised a 'village fete' complete with grass laid down in a residential street. The event, which generated huge media interest, was part of a wider campaign to make streets and neighbourhoods more child-friendly. The Methleys subsequently became one of the first 'home zones' in the UK. Photo: Heads Together Productions.**

This area of new housing in Rijswijk in the Netherlands includes
generous and easily accessible public space and play areas close to
people's homes so that even young children can play outside safely.
Photo: Tim Gill.

Even without such a revolution, it is possible to give greater priority to the creation of communities that foster children's well-being. In the Netherlands and Scandinavia the transport and planning systems have for decades succeeded in creating comparatively child-friendly built environments in these countries. Denmark's approach to road safety shows that this position is not simply the expression of pre-existing child-friendly social values, but is the result of government leadership and vision. Up to the 1970s the country had the highest rates of child road deaths in Western Europe. Consequently in 1976 the Danish Government passed a law that forced local authorities to 'protect children from the dangers of motorised traffic on their way to and from school'. Implementation focused on reducing road danger at source, through highway design and investment in walking and cycling infrastructure. Today Denmark has much higher levels of walking and cycling than the UK, but lower casualty rates.[154]

In the UK, public policy explicitly grounded in notions of child-friendliness is beginning to emerge, although it has a much lower profile than in many European municipalities. Under the leadership of Ken Livingstone and Nicky Gavron, the Mayor and Deputy Mayor of London, the Greater London Authority (GLA) has pursued an explicitly child-friendly planning agenda. The work started in earnest in 2004 with the publication of a comprehensive children's strategy for the city.[155] Its most recent outcome has been the production of planning guidance on outdoor play and informal recreation.[156]

Likewise, a small but growing number of practical community-focused projects to improve streets, parks and play spaces have been making a demonstrable, positive difference to the lives of children, their families and the wider community. One of the most high-profile of such projects is Staiths, a new housing development in Gateshead created by ex-fashion designer Wayne Hemingway, which features play-friendly 'home zone' streets inspired by the Dutch equivalent, the *woonerf*. But there are other examples: the nature playgrounds in Stirling inspired by the Danish landscape architect Helle Nebelong and by the play spaces in Freiburg in Germany; play rangers, a British hybrid of parkkeeper and playworker whose job is to encourage children back into parks and public spaces; safe routes to school projects, another import from Denmark first brought to the UK by the civil engineering charity Sustrans; and some diverse, lightly regulated, welcoming civic spaces like Peace Square in Sheffield or the fountains in the forecourt of Somerset House, London.

Opening up the public realm for children requires strong leadership and a willingness to overcome other imperatives and confront powerful opposing interests. So the urgent demand for new housing, for instance, has to be squared with the need to create liveable streets, compact settlements and high quality, well-managed parks and public spaces. Likewise the motorists' lobby will need to be challenged about its resistance to the widespread introduction of 20 mph speed limits in residential areas: a measure that, given the robust link between vehicle speed and death and serious injury, is a *sine qua non* for child-friendly neighbourhoods. Excessive media influence on policy should also be resisted, whether the default portrayal of young people as yobs or scaremongering about the threat to children from predatory paedophiles.

Children's services: from protection to resilience

Alongside these physical interventions society needs to embrace a philosophy of resilience: an affirmation of the value of children's ability to recover and learn from adverse outcomes, whether these are accidents and injuries, failure, conflict, abuse, neglect, or even tragedy. For example, there should be strong public support for local voluntary and community activities that give children a degree of autonomy and responsibility, and that bring together children and adults. Police, neighbourhood wardens, teachers and other professionals should take a proportionate view about minor public offences and skirmishes involving children. Underpinning all these measures should be a resilient approach to risk, recognising the need for a balance between protection and freedom.

In some sectors the adoption of a philosophy of resilience may be relatively straightforward. But in others, the priorities of different interested parties may make this difficult. Safety regulators, child protection and accident prevention agencies will want to see reductions in accidents, injuries, cases of abuse and neglect and other types of adverse outcome. Those concerned with children's development, learning, health and well-being will have other objectives. Politicians and policymakers may have different priorities again, not least because they may have to weigh the claims of children against those of other sections of the population. In addition to such primary objectives, in a risk-conscious world many individuals and agencies have adopted a secondary objective that reinforces risk aversion: the avoidance of outcomes that may damage their own reputations or prospects.

Chapter 2 described how, in the area of playground safety, experts and agencies have worked together to tackle the spread of risk aversion, and how their work has had a positive impact. This process shows how a sector with entrenched and conflicting views on safety can succeed in building consensus. It has led to a shared sense of direction and a new set of goals that stakeholders at all levels can draw on with confidence since they have the explicit support of leading national agencies. The process of change has been prompted by an agreement that children are not being well-served by the status quo, and that this failure is grounded in confusion about values and goals. Hence a debate has ensued that is explicitly value-based and pluralistic, and has made thoughtful use of the evidence base, not just on playground injuries but also on injuries that happen in other comparable contexts. Consensus has emerged through dialogue rather than being imposed by any one participant.

The process has successfully reframed the problem of playground safety, rejecting philosophies of protection and adopting a philosophy of resilience, by introducing into the debate some broader perspectives and values. Such reframing offers the prospect of progress in other contentious areas of childhood risk.

In policy contexts, the process of reframing could prompt more consensus about the nature and extent of the risks children face, and the role that experience and exposure to risk plays in children's learning and growth, based where possible on evidence as well as on opinion. Such consensus on the nature of different risks allows for greater clarity in defining levels of seriousness, and hence better consideration of the proportionality and impact of interventions. It should also help policymakers to resist political, public and media pressure to find scapegoats and for emotional responses in the aftermath of tragedy. Crucially, professional judgements should be regarded and not undermined by draconian safety initiatives. This would give public services the confidence to resist unjustified calls for interventions from parents and others, and limit their tendency to default to the position that 'he who is most risk averse wins.' Explicit policy statements should allow providers to assert a balanced, realistic assessment of their legal position and responsibilities, providing a robust defence against the threat of claims.

Resilience means finding ways to function in a world in which bad things happen.

So what distinguishes it from fatalism, indifference or negligence? There is no simple answer to this question. Shifting the focus from adults' duty of care to children's agency is challenging, as it can appear, at an extreme, as though children are expected to be responsible for their own safety while society evades responsibility. However, unless children are allowed to take a degree of responsibility and to gain some experience in how to do this, adults in many contexts will feel under ever more pressure to intervene. At worst this could fuel a vicious circle where children's alleged vulnerability provides the rationale for excessive interference, leading to a loss of experiential learning opportunities that in turn leaves children more vulnerable.

There are legitimate questions about the involvement that children themselves might have in the kind of reframing proposed here. It is obviously important to ensure that their perspectives about both risks and benefits are taken into account in debates. Chapter 1 argued that in general children are making plain their wish for greater freedom, autonomy and responsibility for their own safety. Although adults are ultimately responsible for shaping the world children grow up in they should take children's views into account.

With regard to the role of the media, it is hard to regulate or influence decisions when newsworthiness is the prime factor. However, as Chapter 4 noted, the media are increasingly facing in two directions on risk, which may exploit the public's own ambivalence. For example, the threat of abduction from strangers is low and has not increased for decades, but public fears about it are growing, with damaging consequences. The media are undeniably major factors in the escalation of public anxiety yet, as always, are unwilling to accept any responsibility for this.

Questions about the quality of childhood experiences might appear less pressing than such global issues as prosperity, security and sustainability. However, we need to engender a sense that some values cannot simply be related to financial or economic imperatives. In any case, over the long term, progress on all these issues depends critically upon the children of the future growing up as engaged, self-confident, responsible, resilient citizens: people who both feel they have some control over their destinies and are alive to the consequences of their actions. This will only happen if their childhoods include some simple ingredients: frequent, unregulated, self-directed contact with people and places beyond the immediate spheres of family and school, and the chance to learn from their mistakes.

Notes

Chapter 1 **Introduction**

1   BBC website, 13 February 2007: http://news.bbc.co.uk/1/hi/education/6356865.stm; *Denver Post*, 3 September 2007: http://www.denverpost.com/headlines/ci_6788094; *The Age* (Melbourne), 10 July 2006: http://www.theage.com.au/news/national/high-school-children-sick-of-sitting-on-their-classes/2006/07/09/1152383611827.html; Steve Goode, National Play Resource Centre (Ireland) personal communication.

2   Quoted in J. Appleton, *The Case Against Vetting*, published online at: http://www.manifestoclub.com (2006).

3   BBC website, 16 October 2006: http://news.bbc.co.uk/1/hi/england/kent/6057098.stm.

4   BBC website, 29 April 2007: http://news.bbc.co.uk/1/hi/wales/north_west/6605107.stm.

5   H. Cunningham, *The Invention of Childhood* (London, BBC Books, 2006).

6   M. Hillman, J. Adams and J. Whitelegg, *One False Move: A study of children's independent mobility* (London, Policy Studies Institute, 1993); R. Wheway and A. Millward, *Child's Play: Facilitating play on housing estates* (London, Chartered Institute of Housing, 1997).

7   S. Gaster, 'Urban Children's Access to their Neighbourhoods: Changes over three generations' in *Environment and Behaviour*, 23, 1991, pp. 70–85.

8   T. Fotel and T. Thomsen, 'The Surveillance of Children's Mobility' in *Surveillance & Society*, 1(4), 2004, pp. 535–54.

9   Future Foundation, *The Changing Face of Parenting: Professional parenting, information and healthcare* (London, Future Foundation, 2006).

10 P. Blatchford and A. Pellegrini, *The Child at School: Interactions with peers and teachers* (London, Hodder Arnold, 2000); BBC website, 6 May 2007: http://news.bbc.co.uk/1/hi/england/cambridgeshire/6629655.stm.

11 F. Furedi, *Culture of Fear: Risk taking and the morality of low expectation*, 2nd edition (London, Continuum, 2002).

12 D. Wilson, C. Sharp and A. Patterson, *Young People and Crime: Findings from the 2005 offending, crime and justice survey* (London, Home Office, 2006).

13 Crime and Disorder Act 1998. See also Standing Conference on Youth Justice, *Youth Justice: Steps in the right direction* (London, The Children's Society, 2005); available from the Children's Society website: http://www.childrenssociety.org.uk/NR/rdonlyres/B2CB03A2-663C-4470-B1D0-B3F0F10D9AFB/0/Youth_Justice_positionpaper.pdf.

14 D. Lupton, *Risk* (London, Routledge, 1999), Ch 2.

15 Royal Society for the Prevention of Accidents website: http://www.rospa.com/safetyeducation/laser/overview.htm.

16 J. Lindon, *Too Safe For Their Own Good?* (London, National Early Years Network, 1999).

17 D. Jones, *Cotton Wool Kids: Releasing the potential for children to take risks and innovate* (Coventry, HTI, 2007).

18 Lindon (1999), see note 16.

19 J. Lindon, *Understanding Children and Young People: Development from 5–18 years* (London, Hodder Arnold, 2007) gives an authoritative overview.

20 J. Adams, *Risk* (London, UCL Press, 1995), Ch 3.

21 H. Cunningham, *The Guardian*, 20 September 2006.

22 Department for Education and Skills, *Every Child Matters* (London, The Stationery Office, 2003), p. 6.

23   The Children's Society, *Good Childhood? A question for our times* (London, The Children's Society, 2006). See also I. Cole-Hamilton, A. Harrop and C. Street, *Making the Case for Play: Gathering the evidence* (London, National Children's Bureau, 2002).

24   Child Accident Prevention Trust, *Taking Chances: The lifestyles and leisure risk of young people: project summary* (London, Child Accident Prevention Trust, 2002).

25   J. Ward and M. Bayley, 'Young People's Perceptions of "Risk"' in B. Thom, R. Sales and J. Pearce, eds, *Growing up with Risk* (Bristol, Policy Press, 2007).

26   BBC website, 1 March 2005:
news.bbc.co.uk/cbbcnews/hi/newsid_4300000/newsid_4300600/4300681.stm.

27   Better Regulation Task Force, *Better Routes to Redress* (London, Cabinet Office, 2004); Lord Hoffmann, *The Social Cost of Tort Liability* (speech at National Constitution Centre, Philadelphia, USA, 27 June 2005); available from: http://cgood.org/learn-reading-cgpubs-speeches.html.

28   Hoffmann (2005), see note 27.

29   Better Regulation Commission, *Risk, Responsibility and Regulation: Whose risk is it anyway?* (London, Better Regulation Commission, 2006).

30   HSE website: http://www.hse.gov.uk/risk/principles.htm.

31   Lords of Appeal Judgement: Tomlinson (FC) (Original Respondent and Cross-appellant) v. Congleton Borough Council and others (Original Appellants and Cross-respondents), 31 July 2003.

32   Royal Society for the Encouragement of Arts, Manufactures and Commerce (RSA) website: http://www.rsariskcommission.org.

33   The Children's Society (2006), p. 4, see note 23.

34   Hoffmann (2005), see note 27.

Chapter 2 **Playgrounds**

35   P. Heseltine and J. Holborn, *Playgrounds: The planning, design and construction of play environments* (London, Mitchell, 1987).

36   Rob Wheway and Peter Heseltine, personal communication.

37   British Standards Institution, *Play Equipment Intended for Permanent Installation Outdoors: Part 3: Code of practice for installation and maintenance (BS5696)* (London, British Standards Institution, 1979); Department of the Environment, *Children's Playgrounds* (London, Department of the Environment, 1976).

38   *That's Life*, episode broadcast on 27 May 1990.

39   D. Ball, *Playgrounds: Risks, benefits and choices* (Sudbury, Health and Safety Executive, 2002), section 2.1.3.

40   D. Ball, 'Risk and the Demise of Children's Play' in B. Thom, R. Sales and J. Pearce, eds, *Growing up with Risk* (Bristol, Policy Press, 2007), p. 63.

41   Ball (2002), see note 39. There is some uncertainty because in one or two cases it was genuinely difficult to find out exactly what happened.

42   Ball (2007), p. 63, see note 40.

43   Better Regulation Commission (2006), p. 11, see note 29.

44   D. Ball, 'Policy issues and risk-benefit trade-offs of "safer surfacing" for children's playgrounds' in *Accident Analysis and Prevention*, 36, 2004, p. 666 (emphasis in original).

45   Ball (2002), Ch. 4, see note 39.

46   Richard Lumb, Chair, Association of Play Industries, personal communication.

47   Ball (2004), p. 666, see note 44.

48   Cost-benefit analysis for safety surfacing: Ball (2004), see note 44. Cost-benefit analysis for residential traffic calming: R. Elvik, *Cost-Benefit Analysis of Safety Measures for Vulnerable and Inexperienced Road Users: Report no. 435, Work Package 5 of EU-Project PROMISING* (Oslo, Institute of Transport Economics, 1999).

49   Ball (2002), section 5.3, see note 39.

50   P. Heseltine, 'Safety Versus Play Value' in M.L. Christiansen, ed., *Proceedings of Playground Safety* (University Park Pennsylvania, Penn State University, 1995).

51   David Yearley, Head of Playground Safety, Royal Society for the Prevention of Accidents, speaking at Somerset Play Forum Conference, 29 November 2006.

52   Adams (1995), pp. 14–16, see note 20.

53   D. Mok, G. Gore, B. Hagel, E. Mok, H. Magdalinos and B. Pless, 'Risk Compensation in Children's Activities: A pilot study' in *Paediatrics and Child Health*, 9, 2004, pp. 327–30.

54   Ball (2004), p. 664, see note 44.

55   Royal Society for the Prevention of Accidents, *Information Sheet Number 10: EN1176 Playground Equipment Standard* (Birmingham, Royal Society for the Prevention of Accidents, 2004).

56   Advice from the Royal Society for the Prevention of Accidents is not consistent. *Information Sheet Number 9: Dogs on Play Areas* (Birmingham, Royal Society for the Prevention of Accidents, 2004) advises daily inspections, while *Information Sheet Number 6: Code of Good Practice* (2004) advises weekly inspections.

57   Fields in Trust (formerly National Playing Fields Association), *Six Acre Standard* (London, Fields in Trust, 2001).

58   Ball (2002), section 8.4, see note 39.

59   Rob Wheway, personal communication.

60   Common Good website: http://cgood.org/assets/attachments/VoP_—_Selected_Facts.pdf, citing National Electronic Injury Surveillance System, Hospital Emergency Room Treated Injuries: 1998 Estimates from the Consumer Product Safety Commission.

61   P. Howard, *Collapse of the Common Good: How the lawsuit culture undermines our freedom* (New York, Ballantine, 2002), p. 66.

62   In some countries there is anecdotal evidence of rising concerns about playground safety. David Ball quotes a Danish expert who claims that the cost of insurance coverage is leading some municipalities to dismantle play areas and remove equipment – see Ball (2002) note 39, section 7.5.

63   Quoted in P. Harrop, *To Replace Order with Chaos: A brief report on the Growing Adventure study tour* (unpublished, available on request from the Forestry Commission, 2005).

64   Helle Nebelong, speech at 'Designs on Play' conference, Playlink/Portsmouth City Council, Portsmouth, 2002; available from: http://www.freeplaynetwork.org.uk/design/nebelong.htm.

65   Play Safety Forum, *Managing Risk in Play Provision: A position statement* (London, National Children's Bureau, 2002); available from: http://www.ncb.org.uk.

66   Counsel Opinion available from Playlink: http://www.playlink.org.uk.

67   Institute of Sport and Recreation Management Guidance, *ISRM Risk Assessment Guidance for Child Admission Policies* (Policy Statement PS004 09/05).

68   Committé Europeén de Normalisation (CEN), *Playground Equipment and Surfacing – Part 1: General safety requirements and test methods (Draft prEN 1176–1)* (Brussels, CEN, 2006).

69   David Ball, personal communication, 2006.

70   Ball (2007), p. 60, see note 40.

Chapter 3 **The spread of risk averse attitudes to childhood**

71   *Birmingham Mail*, 25 July 2006.

72   BBC website, 28 April 2006: http://news.bbc.co.uk/1/hi/england/manchester/4954826.stm.

73   *Daily Mail*, 23 July 2006.

74   *Birmingham Mail*, 29 November 2004.

75   O. Aldis, *Play Fighting* (New York, Academic Press, 1975).

76   P. Holland, *We Don't Play With Guns Here: War, weapon and superhero play in the early years* (Maidenhead, Open University Press, 2003).

77   N. Freeman and M. Brown, 'Reconceptualizing Rough and Tumble Play: Ban the banning' in *Advances in Early Education and Day Care*, 13, 2004, pp. 219–34; J. Katch, *Under Deadman's Skin: Discovering*

the meaning of children's violent play (Boston, Beacon Press, 2001); Holland (2003), see note 76.

78 P.K. Smith, R. Smees, A.D. Pellegrini and E. Menesini, 'Comparing Pupil and Teacher Perceptions for Playful Fighting, Serious Fighting, and Positive Peer Interaction' in *Play and Culture Studies*, 4, 2002, pp. 235–48; P. Smith and K. Lewis, 'Rough-and-tumble Play, Fighting and Chasing in Nursery School Children' in *Ethology and Sociobiology*, 6, 1985, pp. 175–81.

79 J. Margo, M. Dixon, N. Pearce and H. Reed, *Freedom's Orphans* (London, Institute for Public Policy Research, 2006).

80 V. Besag, 'The Playground' in M. Elliot, ed., *Bullying: A practical guide to coping for schools* (Harlow, Pearson Education, 2002).

81 House of Commons Education and Skills Committee, *Bullying: Third report of session 2006–07* (London, The Stationery Office, 2007), p. 8 and Ev 6; J. Deakin, 'Dangerous People, Dangerous Places: The nature and location of young people's victimisation and fear' in *Children & Society*, 20 (5), 2006, pp. 376–90.

82 Dr K.B. Everard, Trustee and former Chair, Central Herts YMCA, personal communication.

83 Department for Education and Skills, *Final Regulatory Impact Assessment for the Post-Bichard Vetting and Barring Scheme* (London, Department for Education and Skills, 2006).

84 DfES (2006), p. 5, see note 83.

85 P. Cawson, C. Wattam, S. Brooker and G. Kelly, *Child Maltreatment in the United Kingdom: A study of the prevalence of abuse and neglect: executive summary* (London, National Society for the Prevention of Cruelty to Children, 2000).

86 S.J. Creighton and G. Tissier, *Child Killings in England and Wales* (London, National Society for the Prevention of Cruelty to Children, 2003); available from: http://www.nspcc.org.uk/inform/research/briefings/childkillingsinenglandandwales_ifega45948.html.

87 J. Appleton, *The Case Against Vetting* (2006), published online at: http://www.manifestoclub.com/files/the%20case%20against%20vetting.pdf.

88 M. Power, *The Risk Management of Everything* (London, Demos, 2004), p. 42.

89 BBC website, 21 May 2006: http://news.bbc.co.uk/1/hi/uk/5001624.stm.

90 Appleton (2006), pp. 15–16, see note 87.

91 *The Times*, 18 September 2006.

92 J. Adams, '7/7: *What* kills you matters, *not* numbers'; available from: http://www.socialaffairsunit.org.uk/blog/archives/000512.php.

93 *The Times*, 19 July 2006.

94 Home Office Research Development and Statistics Directorate, personal communication.

95 Creighton and Tissier (2003), see note 86.

96 F. Furedi, *Paranoid Parenting: Abandon your anxieties and be a good parent* (London, Allen Lane, 2001).

97 F. Brookman and M. Maguire, *Reducing Homicide: A review of the possibilities* (London, Home Office, 2003), p. 16, n. 16.

98 J. Silverman and D. Wilson, *Innocence Betrayed: Paedophilia, the media and society* (Cambridge, Polity, 2002), pp. 183–4.

99 B. Gallagher, M. Bradford and K. Pease, 'The Sexual Abuse of Children by Strangers: Its extent, nature and victims' characteristics' in *Children & Society*, 16, 2002, pp. 346–59.

100 Deakin (2006), see note 81.

101 K. Kendall-Tackett, L. Williams and D. Finkelhor, 'Impact of Sexual Abuse on Children: A review and synthesis of recent empirical studies' in *Psychological Bulletin*, 113, 1993, pp. 164–80. Also Silverman and Wilson (2002), Ch. 3, see note 98.

102 See for instance K. Ginsburg, 'The Importance of Play in Promoting Healthy Child Development and Maintaining Strong Parent-Child Bonds' in *Paediatrics*, 119, 2007, pp. 182–91; available from: http://www.aap.org/pressroom/playFINAL.pdf (2006).

103 Mental Health Foundation, *Bright Futures* (London, Mental Health Foundation, 1999).

104 J. Jacobs, *The Death and Life of Great American Cities,* Vintage Books Edition (New York, Vintage, 1992), p. 82.

105 BBC website, 23 March 2006: http://news.bbc.co.uk/1/hi/england/coventry_warwickshire/4837614.stm.

106 Kidscape, *Keep Them Safe* (London, Kidscape, 2001); available from: http://www.kidscape.org.uk.

107 Protective Behaviours UK website: http://www.protectivebehaviours.co.uk/AboutPBs.htm.

108 S. Livingstone and M. Bober, *UK Children Go Online: Final report of key project findings* (London, London School of Economics and Political Science, 2005).

109 Ofcom, *The Communications Market 2007 Nations and Regions: Communications markets across the United Kingdom* (London, Ofcom, 2007), p. 51.

110 H. Green and C. Hannon, *Their Space: Education for a digital generation* (London, Demos, 2007).

111 Child Exploitation and Online Protection (CEOP) Centre, *Strategic Review 2006–7* (London, CEOP, 2007).

112 CEOP (2007), p. 7, see note 111. This figure is, according to the report, 'based on a partial sample of 6,000 respondents' although the survey methodology is not stated.

113 Cunningham (2006), p. 230, see note 5.

114 Monthly Prime Minister's press conference, 3 September 2007. See the 10 Downing Street website: http://www.pm.gov.uk/output/Page13034.asp.

115 A. Millwood Hargrave and S. Livingstone, *Harm and Offence in Media Content: A review of the empirical literature* (Bristol, Intellect Press, 2006). Abbreviated version available from: http://www.lse.ac.uk/collections/media@lse/whosWho/soniaLivingstone.htm.

116 Millwood Hargrave and Livingstone (2006), p. 16, see note 115.

117 Millwood Hargrave and Livingstone (2006), p. 200, see note 115.

118 Millwood Hargrave and Livingstone (2006), p. 17, see note 115.

119 Millwood Hargrave and Livingstone (2006), p. 17 see note 115.

120 Millwood Hargrave and Livingstone (2006), p. 18, see note 115.

121 Livingstone and Bober (2005), p. 25, see note 108.

122 Livingstone and Bober (2005), p. 26, see note 108.

Chapter 4 **Who is to blame?**

123 Future Foundation, *The Changing Face of Parenting: Professional parenting, information and healthcare* (London, Future Foundation, 2006).

124 UNICEF, *A league table of child deaths by injury in rich nations*, Innocenti Report Card 2 (Florence, UNICEF Innocenti Research Centre, 2001); available from: http://www.unicef-icdc.org.

125 The following sections draw on Cunningham (2006), see note 5, and publicly available statistics from the General Household Survey and Social Trends. The perspective is influenced by Robert Putnam's work on social capital, especially R. Putnam, *Bowling Alone: The collapse and revival of American community* (New York, Simon & Schuster, 2000), and the work of Jane Jacobs, see note 104.

126 *Independent on Sunday*, 24 October 2004.

127 CLEAPSS, *Surely That's Banned?* (London, Royal Society of Chemistry, 2005); National Advisory Committee on Creative and Cultural Education, *All Our Futures: Creativity, culture and education* (London, Department for Culture, Media and Sport, 1999); National Heart Forum, *A Review of the Impact of the Law on the Promotion of Physical Activity for the Department of Health in England* (Unpublished, 2004).

128 House of Commons Education and Skills Committee, *Education Outside the Classroom: Second report of session 2004–05* (London, HMSO, 2005).

129 Forest Education Initiative website: http://www.foresteducation.org/.

130 S. Bond, *Why do Forest Schools?* (Forest Schools East, undated); available from: http://www.forest-schools-east.org/detail.htm.

131 Susannah Podmore, Forestry Commission, personal communication.

132 L. O'Brien and R. Murray, *A Marvellous Opportunity for Children to Learn: A participatory evaluation of Forest School in England and Wales* (Farnham, Forest Research, 2006).

133 Blatchford and Pellegrini (2000), see note 10.

134 BBC website, 6 May 2007: http://news.bbc.co.uk/1/hi/england/cambridgeshire/6629655.stm.

135 Antony Pellegrini, speech at Common Good conference, Washington DC, 31 May 2006 (summarising the findings of A. Pellegrini, P. Blatchford, K. Kato and E. Baines, 'A short-time longitudinal study of children's playground games in primary school: Implications for adjustment to school and social adjustment in the USA and the UK' in *Social Development*, 13, 2004, pp. 107–23).

136 NASUWT website: http://www.nasuwt.org.uk/Templates/Internal.asp?NodeID=71684.

137 Playlink, *Play at School* (London, Playlink, 1999).

138 J. Lindon, *Understanding Child Development: Linking theory and practice* (London, Hodder Arnold, 2005), p. 132.

139 Creative Partnerships, *This Much We Know... Creative Partnerships approach and impact* (London, Arts Council England, 2007).

140 Guide Association, *Reality Checks: Risk* (London, Guide Association, 2006).

141 Play Wales, *Playwork Principles* (undated); available from: http://www.playwales.org.uk/page.asp?id=50.

142 P. Moss and P. Petrie, *From Children's Services to Children's Spaces* (London, Taylor and Francis, 2002); Barnardo's, *More School, Less Play? The role of play in the Extended School in Denmark and England* (Barkingside, Barnardo's, 2006); available from: http://www.barnardos.org.uk/more_school_less_play_the_role_of_play_in_the_extended_school_in _denmark_and_england.pdf.

143 C. Wardle, '"It Could Happen to You": The move towards "personal" and "societal" narratives in newspaper coverage of child murder, 1930–2000' in *Journalism Studies*, 7, 2006, pp. 515–33.

144 Andrew Marr, *My Trade: A short history of British journalism* (London, Macmillan, 2004).

145 *Daily Mail*, 30 May 2000.

146 Children's Workforce Development Council website: http://www.cwdcouncil.org.uk.

147 Children's Workforce Development Council, *Induction Standards* (Leeds, Children's Workforce Development Council, 2006).

Chapter 5 **Beyond risk aversion**

148 Better Regulation Commission (2006), p. 37, see note 27.

149 UNICEF, *Child poverty in perspective: An overview of child well-being in rich countries*, Innocenti Report Card 7 (Florence, UNICEF Innocenti Research Centre, 2007).

150 S. Collishaw, B. Maughan, R. Goodman and A .Pickles, 'Time trends in adolescent mental health' in *Journal of Child Psychology and Psychiatry*, 45 (8), 2004, pp. 1350–62.

151 Mental Health Foundation, *Bright Futures* (London, Mental Health Foundation, 1999).

152 June McKerrow quoted online at: http://www.sirc.org/media/mediaaugust1399.html.

153 For information on the human scale schools movement see: http://www.hse.org.uk.

154 T. Andersen, 'Safe routes to school in Odense, Denmark' in R. Tolley, ed., *The Greening of Urban Transport: Planning for walking and cycling in Western cities*, 2nd edition (Chichester, Wiley, 1997).

155 *Making London Better for All Children and Young People: The Mayor's Children and Young People's Strategy* (London, Greater London Authority, 2004).

156 *Providing for Children and Young People's Play and Informal Recreation: The London Plan (Spatial Development Strategy for Greater London), draft supplementary planning guidance* (London, Greater London Authority, 2006).

Select bibliography and further reading

The following publications and resources are a selection of some of the more accessible material referred to in the text.

J. Adams, *Risk* (London, UCL Press, 1995).

Better Regulation Commission, *Risk, Responsibility and Regulation: Whose risk is it anyway?* (London, Better Regulation Commission, 2006).

P. Blatchford and A. Pellegrini, *The Child at School: Interactions with peers and teachers* (London, Hodder Arnold, 2000).

H. Cunningham, *The Invention of Childhood* (London, BBC Books, 2006).

Free Play Network website: http://www.freeplaynetwork.org.uk.

F. Furedi, *Paranoid Parenting: Abandon your anxieties and be a good parent* (London, Allen Lane, 2001).

B. Gallagher, M. Bradford and K. Pease, 'The Sexual Abuse of Children by Strangers: Its extent, nature and victims' characteristics' in *Children & Society*, 16, 2002, pp. 346–59.

M. Hillman, J. Adams and J. Whitelegg, *One False Move: A study of children's independent mobility* (London, Policy Studies Institute, 1993).

Lord Hoffmann, *The Social Cost of Tort Liability* (speech at National Constitution Centre, Philadelphia, USA, 27 June 2005); available from: http://cgood.org/learn-reading-cgpubs-speeches.html.

P. Holland, *We Don't Play With Guns Here: War, weapon and superhero play in the early years* (Maidenhead, Open University Press, 2003).

J. Lindon, *Too Safe For Their Own Good?* (London, National Early Years Network, 1999).

J. Lindon, *Understanding Children and Young People: Development from 5–18 years* (London, Hodder Arnold, 2007).

S. Livingstone and M. Bober, *UK Children Go Online: Final report of key project findings* (London, London School of Economics and Political Science, 2005).

Play Safety Forum, *Managing Risk in Play Provision*: *A position statement* (London, National Children's Bureau, 2002); available from http://www.ncb.org.uk.

M. Power, *The Risk Management of Everything* (London, Demos, 2004); available from: http://www.demos.co.uk.

Protective Behaviours UK website: http://www.protectivebehaviours.co.uk.

Royal Society for the Encouragement of Arts, Manufactures and Commerce (RSA) Risk Commission website: http://www.rsariskcommission.org.

J. Silverman and D. Wilson, *Innocence Betrayed: Paedophilia, the media and society* (Cambridge, Polity, 2002).

B. Thom, R. Sales and J. Pearce, eds, *Growing up with Risk* (Bristol, Policy Press, 2007).

UNICEF, *A league table of child deaths by injury in rich nations,* Innocenti Report Card 2 (Florence, UNICEF Innocenti Research Centre, 2001); available from http://www.unicef-irc.org.

C. Wardle, '"It Could Happen to You": The move towards "personal" and "societal" narratives in newspaper coverage of child murder, 1930–2000' in *Journalism Studies*, 7, 2006, pp. 515–33.

Photographic acknowledgements

Nils Norman is an artist working across the disciplines of public art, architecture and urban planning. He has completed two large commissions for Platform for Art, London 2007; participated in Global Cities, Tate Modern 2007; participated in the British Art Show 2005, the Venice Biennale 2003 and the Havana Biennale 2002; completed residencies at Camden Arts Centre and the University of Chicago, USA, both in 2005; and is the author of three books, including *An Architecture of Play: A Survey of London's Adventure Playgrounds* (Four Corners, 2004). He is currently a Professor at the Royal Danish Art Academy, Copenhagen.

Nils Norman would like to thank the following for help with the photographs: Emily Pethick, Robin Sutcliffe, Shoko, Kanade and Kotone Ohmura, Tomoko Takada, Hitoshi Shimamura, Nana Saito, Hitomi Kobayashi, everyone at Mitsumata Adventure Playground, Tanuki Yama, Ko Senda, Sean Snyder, Frode Svane, Florian Zeyfang, Lucas Kimber and Marta Nowicka.

Photographs by Nils Norman: front cover and pages 27, 33, 34, 67, 71.
Photographs by Tim Gill: pages 11, 18, 40, 50, 80.
Photograph on page 2, Virginia Sullivan; page 58, John Birdsall Social Issues Photo Library (www.johnbirdsall.co.uk); and page 78, Heads Together Productions.